JÜRGEN
MOLTMANN

THE
EXPERIMENT
HOPE

Edited, translated,
with a Foreword by
M. DOUGLAS MEEKS

FORTRESS PRESS
Philadelphia

Library of Congress Catalog Card Number 74–26339

ISBN–0–8006–0407–5

4634L74   Printed in the United States of America   1–407

Contents

Contents

Translator's Note

Several of the essays in this book have appeared previously in English. "Christian Theology and Its Problems Today" and "Bringing Peace to a Divided World" appeared in *Theology Digest* (Winter 1971 and Winter 1972); "Where There Is Hope, There Is Religion" and "Introduction to the 'Theology of Hope'" were printed in the *Kalamazoo College Review* (No. 3, 1970); "The Crucified God and the Apathetic Man," under the title, "The Crucified God," and "Political Theology" appeared in *Theology Today* (April 1974 and April 1971); the essay "Racism and the Right to Resist" was translated by the World Council of Churches, and "Ernst Bloch and Hope without Faith" was included, in very different form, in *Concilium* (1966).

This translation has been prepared with keen awareness of the insensitivities explicit and implicit in the frequent use of the term *man*. Unfortunately, the German *Mensch* does not lend itself to unambiguous English. It has not been possible to solve this problem with consistency or felicity. It is hoped that the reader will understand that the term is here used in its generic sense and with no exclusivist overtones.

I am pleased to acknowledge the helpful suggestions I received from the following persons who read portions of the translations: Drs. Gerhard M. Martin, Scott H. Hendrix, Lowell Zuck, and Mr. David Watson.

Foreword

by M. DOUGLAS MEEKS

Ten years after the German publication of *Theology of Hope*, there can be no doubt that Jürgen Moltmann's theology will have a tremendous creative influence on the future of theology and the church. In both the United States and Germany the theological fronts shifted rapidly during the 1960s. Of the countless movements and "new directions" announced in that period of internal and external turmoil, Moltmann's theology is one of the very few which is still relevant to the practice of Christians in the world. This is due in part to the amazing internal development of his theology in relation to the changing historical conditions of the last decade. But the real reason lies in the integrity of his reflection in dialectically relating biblical, systematic, and politico-ethical concerns. A theology which prizes experience higher than faith will always shine brightly in its reflection of the times, but will soon fade with those times. A theology which also understands that faith creates experience, however, will have a decisive and critical part to play in that history-making process which is the Christian Apostolate. The subject, the substance, and the text of Moltmann's theology account for its continuing power in calling Christianity to the responsibility and joy of its peculiar destiny.

Moltmann's theology is developing into a full-blown systematic endeavor. In coming years it will surely elicit the admiration and expectancy which the church held for the theologies of Barth, Bultmann, and the Niebuhrs in past generations. The lasting value of the essays collected here is the development of Moltmann's "theology of hope" (1) in a new historical and social situation and (2) according to the internal fermenting of its subject matter. From the beginning Moltmann viewed his theology as *experimental*.[1] He didn't mean this in the sense that theology should try something new every time the winds change. He was rather proposing that theology find a practical correspondence to the fundamentally experimental relationship of God with the world and of the Christian mission with history. "Experiment," in this sense, belongs to the language of promise and covenant. It points to a reality in which all things are open to the future and on the move and whose final transformation is already expected and provisionally embodied in the present. In the midst of God's experiment with his creation and Christianity's experiment with the other history-making events of human history only one thing is utterly certain and beyond all doubt: the faithfulness of God to himself and to his Word of promise. In continuity with the promissory traditions of the Bible, such a theological perspective is able to live through time precisely because it does not adapt to the times.

The new historical situation which appeared at the end of the sixties and the beginning of the seventies was characterized by a feeling that the processes of secularization and democratization had aborted and that the great technological and bureaucratic systems of both liberal and revolutionary humanism had failed. There was no longer an atmosphere of excited optimism about the future, such as many thought had stimulated the "theology of hope." Rather a deep despair and uncertainty led many people to new forms of escapism and resignation. The human prospect (Heilbroner) did not correspond to a mood of hope about the future. The substance of the theology of hope, however, had never neatly corresponded to the futuristic expectations of the early sixties. The text of the theology of hope speaks of the resurrection of the *crucified one*. It is a text which understands and experiences the negative, which knows itself to be out of joint with the times, especially the optimistic times. Some of the themes which come to the fore in these essays may seem at first to be far removed or even contradictory to the theology of hope. But these new phases of the experiment of hope do not represent a refusal or even a correction of the theology of hope as much as a development of certain more or less latent elements of the theology of hope. The first stages of the theology of hope emphasized the world-openness of theology and the church; the later stages have focused on their self-identity. In this way Moltmann's developing theology has quickened theology's age-old dialectic between relevance and identity.

These essays can also be viewed as connecting links between Moltmann's two major books, *Theology of Hope* and *The Crucified God* (1974, first published in German in 1972).[2] If we look for a basic structure in the development of Moltmann's theology, we can see clearly its trinitarian nature from the beginning. All three trinitarian moments have been present throughout, but it is possible to understand *Theology of Hope* as an experiment in conceiving the history of Israel and the Christ event from the perspective of a thoroughgoing eschatological conception of God. The act of God in the resurrection was clearly the focus of this stage. Likewise one can understand *The Crucified God* as an experiment in understanding God from a thoroughgoing christological perspective of the crucified Christ. Here the cross moves to the central place of the dialectic. In both stages one can see the emerging dialectic between this eschatological Christology and this christological eschatology from which derives a theology of the process of the Spirit and of the church. From the perspective of this final stage the dynamic of Pentecost drives forward the dialectic. Thus the moments of the internal dialectic and the external development of Moltmann's theology are resurrection, cross, and Pentecost. In this sense the experiment of the theology of hope reveals itself as a trinitarian process.[3] More specifically the present collection of writings shows the growth of Moltmann's thought in the direction of a trinitarian theology which is focused in the theology of the cross and aims at a *pathic* anthropology. Moltmann had claimed formerly that faith has the priority and hope the *prius* in the logic of Christian theology.[4] More recently he has been concerned to show the implications of faith and hope for a suffering love.

The unity and interrelationship of these essays can be seen in terms of four stages or movements in the unfolding of Moltmann's theology: (1) the eschatological horizon of Christian theology, (2) the liberating mission of the church in the world, (3) the christological criterion and content of Christian theology, and (4) the historical anthropology of the pathic human being.

I

The methodology of *Theology of Hope* was to consider every aspect of Christian theology from the eschatological perspective of God's future and his coming kingdom.[5] That volume criticized modern views of revelation, history, Christ, and the church and demonstrated that they had been determined by theology's choice of subjectivity as its own special modality, free from the objectifying methods of the natural and historical sciences. The upshot of this choice was that theology and the church lost their historical and social bearings. Modern theology had tended to reduce faith to internal self-identity in the immediacy of the moment and love to trans-historical and trans-social interaction of homogenous individuals beyond the objective political and economic conditions of society. Moltmann demonstrated a way of opening up faith and love to genuine historical existence in the secular and political world by vivifying both with that Christian hope which sees everything as subject to the risk and possibilities of history in view of the horizon of God's coming sovereignty.

From this perspective revelation has the shape of promise. Knowledge of God is not based on the natural orders and processes, on the self-consciousness of the self, or on the notion of God's eternal being. Rather it is viewed historically as at once disclosing God's faithfulness and man's calling to historical tasks. This biblical view of revelation and of God's relationship to the future demanded a new conception of reality as history. God's faithful promise and man's response to God's covenant faithfulness are both "stretched out" historically, so to speak. The realization of God's faithfulness from promise to fulfillment takes time and man must live through time in expectation of the fulfillment and in obedient response to God's command, which is the reverse side of his promise. Instead of eliminating the categories of risk and danger, of the new and of historical transformation, as has most of modern theology, Christian hope is called to embrace them in its missionary search for the concrete possibilities of new obedience to God's rule.

The hope of this mission lives out of God's act in raising the crucified Jesus. Jesus' whole life and destiny are seen in terms of God's ultimate lordship. Thus it is possible to appreciate the

precursory and provisional dimension of the Christ event itself.
It also has a promissory character. In his destruction of death in
the dead Jesus, God has entered into the Godforsakenness of this
world and has promised life and new creation for all things. God
has not yet accomplished everything in Jesus Christ. Rather he
has taken up Christ into his own future. This has the effect of
making Christians aware that they are living "between the times"
and that they are called to fill up the times and places of this
world with proclamation of God's faithfulness and of the beginning
of his new future here and now. The church thus cannot be viewed
as an end in itself but is called to serve in bodily (i.e., social and
historical) obedience the requirements of God's kingdom in the
world.

II

The eschatological emphasis of Moltmann's theology was from
its inception combined with an "ethic of hope" which Moltmann,
together with others, later called "political theology." The sphere
of new obedience for the Christian is politics, that is, the comprehensive situation of power relationships among human beings
and between human beings and nature. The quality of human
life is decided in the value-oriented context of polity in which
there are new power factors but little indication of a growing
human maturity. The Bible should be read precisely in such
political situations of suffering and possibility. Moltmann's "political hermeneutic" showed that the messianic-missionary traditions of the Bible become understandable and practicable when
they are read by persons who are standing in the same direction
of righteousness and holding the same intention of liberation as
the original initiatives which gave rise to these traditions.[6] Political
theology thus begins with the criticism of theology itself. With
the help of certain critical tools of the Frankfurt School of Social
Criticism Moltmann argued that every theologian should be
aware of the interests which he or she is serving. Every theologian
should ask: For whom is my theology good? Which persons and
which power structures does it serve? Instead of asking the question of Bultmann, "What sense does it make to speak of God?"
political theology raised the question, "What practical difference

does it make socially and politically to speak of God?" Instead of
beginning with demythologizing and form criticism as applied to
the object of Christian theology, the theologian should begin with
a criticism of his or her own social and political context.[7] Only
then can he or she move to the second task of helping the church
become aware of its own ties with society, with politics, and with
particular economic systems. A church which is freed for faithfulness to its Lord will then be a free space in which persons can
be empowered to criticize and transform the idolatry which de-
humanizes politics.

In order to see how Moltmann has developed these themes in
their contemporary and historical frameworks, the reader can
refer to the programmatic essay "Political Theology." In "Ernst
Bloch and Hope without Faith," Moltmann articulates his appre-
ciation as well as criticism of Bloch's philosophy of hope. Moltmann's political theology and his theology of the cross have
developed in dialogue with atheist humanism which denies God
because of the suffering of the world or, as Bloch says, denies God
for "the sake of God." Atheist humanists and Christians stand together in the solidarity of suffering and both know about the contradiction between God and reality. A perspective on the historical
background of political theology is to be found in the essays "The
Ethic of Calvinism" and "The Theological Basis of Human Rights
and of the Liberation of Man." One can observe clearly the ground
of Moltmann's political theology in the Reformed emphasis on
obedience to Christ's lordship in all dimensions of life. His
political theology has proceeded in a concrete struggle against the
"law tendency" and the submissive mentality of German theology
and church life. The concrete context of his theology, however,
extends to the ecumenical scene. Through the ecumenical framework his theology has been immediately involved in the liberation
struggles not only of Europe and the Americas but also of Africa
and Asia (see "Racism and the Right to Resistance").

The great strength of Moltmann's developing political theology
is his emphasis on the multidimensionality of human oppression
and liberation. "Bringing Peace to a Divided World" shows that
working exclusively within any one vicious circle of dehumaniza-
tion may actually increase oppression or exploitation in another

vicious circle. The liberation of human beings in their full historical conditionedness depends on struggling simultaneously
against racial and sexual alienation, economic exploitation, political oppression, and the destruction of nature. Moltmann's careful
historical and systematic reflection on violence and resistance
makes an important material contribution to the increasingly
urgent debate on the transformation of power. The necessity as
well as the possibility of relating systematic theology and social
ethics becomes patent in these essays.

Perhaps the most interesting story in the development of Moltmann's theology is the way in which his political theology led him
to deeper dimensions of his systematic theology. If political theology is to be more than a mere religious sanction for social
criticism, one has to ask what makes a theology specifically
Christian.

III

The world-openness of the process of identification in political
theology led increasingly to Moltmann's concern with the criterion
of identity in Christian faith. It became more and more clear to
him that the heart of political theology and liberation theology
must be the criticism of idols and the radical transformation of
values. And this means that the universality of Christian hope
must be constantly related to the particularity of Christian faith.
"There is not a true *theology of hope* which is not first of all a
theology of the cross." Whereas in *Theology of Hope* Moltmann
developed doctrines of God, Christ, and history from the eschatological horizon of God's power and justice as seen in the resurrection, in his theology of the cross he has worked out doctrines of
God, Christ, and man from the perspective of God's suffering and
love in the passion and death of Jesus. The focus here, however,
is not simply on the criterion of identity for Christian faith, but
also on the ground and source of Christian faith. Thus the "theology of the cross" is not a correction of the "theology of hope"
so much as it is an unfolding of the basic dialectic between cross
and resurrection with which Moltmann's theology began.

If the crucifixion of the resurrected one is the criterion and
content of Christian faith, we have a specific vantage point for

understanding the Incarnation and the Trinity. The short article "Jewish and Christian Messianism" shows how crucial Moltmann's dialogue with Jewish theologians has been for his doctrines of God and Christ.[8] The process of Jesus includes his being condemned not only by the religious leaders of his own people and the political authorities of the *Pax Romana* but also by his Father in the cross. But this fact is already at the heart of the proclamation of the good news because it means that no human being can be outside of Jesus' own suffering and abandonment.

The suffering of the event of the cross is not extraneous to God himself. In the abandonment of the Son there seems to be an infinite separation between the Father and the Son and yet in this separation the Father suffers the death of the Son. On the other hand, there is an infinite unity between the Father and the Son in their intention of salvation "for us." As a result we can speak of a community of sacrifice between Father and Son. Reflecting on God's suffering in the event of the cross will mean taking up into the Trinity the full historical Godforsakenness of Jesus as well as God's own suffering. Thus as Moltmann claims in "The Crucified God and the Apathetic Man":

If we understand the doctrine of the Trinity as a description of the God-situation in the cross of Christ, then it is no longer speculation. It is nothing less than a summary of the passion story. The material principle of the doctrine of the Trinity is the cross. The formal principle of the theology of the cross is the doctrine of the Trinity.

Moltmann's emphasis on the cross as the principal constitutive event in the relationship between the Father, the Son, and the Holy Spirit is leading to fascinating new reflections on the internal life and history of God himself.

IV

These reflections are the ground for the development of Moltmann's pathic anthropology and ethic.[9] The first stages of the "ethic of hope" emphasized the theological elements which could motivate people to activity and encourage them to social transformation. His more recent anthropological and ethical reflection, while not leaving these themes behind, is more concerned to show

how a pathic view of humanity is drawn from the conception of God's own suffering. On the practical level he is searching for a more realistic, historical understanding of power. Power which is not able to suffer is not able to live through time, to maintain its interest, and to deal with its failures and disappointments. Here Moltmann is struggling against the growing apathy of our society. He means by apathy not only human indifference and lack of participation but more particularly the fundamental inability to love. Moltmann's earlier thought demonstrated how faith and hope ground love. Here the ethical implications of this are drawn out by showing how love which is born in the cross is related to power and justice. Moltmann understands love as the power of suffering through time with persistent passion for justice in the face of death and evil. "The Humanity of Living and Dying" is a good example of the application and possibilities of this pathic ethic. Like the other essays of this book it can be viewed both as "result" and as a further provocation to the ongoing experiment of hope.

NOTES TO FOREWORD

1. See Moltmann's "Antwort auf die Kritik der Theologie der Hoffnung," in *Diskussion über die Theologie der Hoffnung,* ed. W.-D. Marsch (Munich: Chr. Kaiser, 1967), pp. 201–238.
2. *The Crucified God* (New York: Harper & Row, 1974).
3. In this respect, as well as others, Moltmann's theology shows striking parallels to the developing thought of H. Richard Niebuhr. See James W. Fowler, *To See the Kingdom: The Theological Vision of H. Richard Niebuhr* (Nashville: Abingdon, 1974).
4. *Theology of Hope,* trans. James W. Leitch (New York: Harper & Row, 1967).
5. For the following see my *Origins of the Theology of Hope* (Philadelphia: Fortress Press, 1974).
6. See Jürgen Moltmann, *Religion, Revolution, and the Future,* trans. M. Douglas Meeks (New York: Charles Scribner's Sons, 1969), pp. 83–107.
7. Cf. Jürgen Moltmann, "Theologische Kritik der politischen Religion," in *Kirche im Prozess der Aufklärung,* ed. J. Metz, J. Moltmann, W. Oemüller (Munich/Mainz: Kaiser/Grunewald, 1970).
8. Franz Rosenzweig's thought has been a primary source of the spirit and shape of Moltmann's theology from the beginning. In these essays his indebtedness to Abraham Heschel, Gershom Scholem, and other Jewish theologians also becomes clear.
9. Cf. Jürgen Moltmann, *Man,* trans. John Sturdy (Philadelphia: Fortress Press, 1974).

I.

Christian Theology
and Its Problems Today

The theologian is a strange creature. He is obliged to talk about God who is unconditionally present to all men in all times and all places, but he is himself only a man who is limited in his capacities and who is conditioned in his views by his own tradition and culture. In this essay on Christian theology and some of its problems, I would like to write about what is common to all of us in Europe, America, Asia, and Africa, about what we are questioning together and what we have been commissioned to do together. But, as I am not an angel but only a man, my perspectives are very limited. They are white, European, middle-class, and Protestant; they come out of the twentieth entury (I hope); and they are ultimately determined by my personal experiences and private limitations. Therefore, for theologians from other lands and churches and cultures, they can serve only as suggestions to others to look in the same direction from their points of view toward the God who has brought us into his community and who will bring us to a better community with one another.

Thesis 1. *Christian theology is faced today with a twofold crisis. Rapid social and cultural change has brought it to a crisis of its meaning for the world. And the more theology tries to be relevant to the social crises of its society, the more deeply it is itself drawn into the crisis of its own Christian identity. This twofold crisis is called the "identity-involvement dilemma." But it is not a product of the twentieth century, nor is it in fact a dilemma. It is of the essence of Christian theology from its inception that it investigates ever anew its relevance to the world and its identity in Christ.*

Our efforts toward a renewal of theology and the churches began with the vague uneasy feeling that Christianity had lost contact with its environment and had become irrelevant and no longer worthy of humanity's faith. Many students abandoned the study of theology, and studied sociology, psychology, or revolution, because they felt that they could thereby contribute more toward resolving the problems of today. The old theology they once learned seems to them a "fossil theology." Fundamentalism petrifies the Bible, conservatism makes liturgy inflexible, and Christian morality becomes icebound by rigid legalism.

Sensing theology's loss of contact, many theologians have drawn up new theologies related to the practical areas of modern life—to socialization, industrialization, and the revolution of rising expectations in the Third World. They have provided Christian theology with the characteristics of the context in which they think theology must be made relevant. Thus there arose a series of new movements such as modern theology, indigenous theology, existential theology, linguistic theology, political theology, the theology of secularization, of revolution, of liberation, and so on. Because the relevance of Christian theology had become uncertain, each movement sought for a modern, relevant, practical, and interesting theology for the contemporary world.

But what is Christian about theology in these perspectives? Does theology not lose its Christian identity when it strives to adapt itself "to the winds of time"?

Quite similar movements arose in our churches. A church that cannot change becomes a fossil church. It becomes an unimportant sect on the edge of a rapidly changing and progressive society. Men run away from such a church. Only the old, the tired, and the resigned retain their membership. And so, while the church presses on with her religious activity, namely, of arousing and maintaining the faith, progressive Christians strive with equal force for social involvement in current class and racial struggles and for political action for a world with more justice and freedom. "If someone wants to be a Christian, don't send him into the churches, but into the slums," they say. "That is where he will find Christ."

Will this departure from the traditional and established churches lead to a complete separation from the church? Will the progressives found a new church, or are they wandering into "no man's land"? Are they not often swallowed up by other groups and political parties, which are peculiarly effective in organizing political activity? Anyone who has taken part in such movements of relevant action will, sooner or later, experience a crisis of identity. For if social and political involvement is necessary because of our faith, then what is specifically Christian in this involvement? Not social criticism, for this is waged also by socialists and Marxists. Not personal risk, for non-Christians also rebel, and often better than Christians. If Christianity mingles with social and political movements until it becomes completely identified with them, then the church will again become what is called a religion of society—not a conservative religion, to be sure, but a progressive religion of a future and perhaps better society. But can the church of the crucified man from Nazareth ever become a political religion, without forgetting him and losing its identity?

The times are changing, and society and men in society are caught up in rapid change. A modern theology which desires merely to be a "contextual theology" is often similar to a chameleon that always assumes the colors of its environment. This "chameleon theology" is no better than a fossil theology, for a chameleon changes the color of its skin in order to adapt itself and hide among the leaves. But Christian theology should not adapt itself in order to hide; it is required rather to reveal what is specifically its own in the changing times. Christian theology should rather be an "anti-chameleon theology," and that means displaying colors which contrast with its environment.

A fossil belongs in a museum, a chameleon in its natural environment. Christians, however, are required, as Christians, to be *people of their age* and, as people of their age, to be *Christians*. Only when they have the courage to be and act different from others can they be for others (Bonhoeffer) and mean something to others. They are, however, only different when they become identified in faith with Jesus, who was foolishness for the wise, a stumbling block for the pious, and a troublemaker for the powerful, and therefore was crucified. If God raised him and made him his Christ, then only in the following of Jesus is the divine power of liberation granted to men. The question is not whether the church is modern, relevant, and interesting, but how the crucified one is

Lord, as the leader of life and of freedom, and, consequently, how Christians follow him and hope in him.

Christian theology finds both its identity and its relevance in the *cross of Christ*. It finds its *identity* as Christian theology there; for his cross separates faith from superstition, as well as from unbelief. His cross separates theology from other religions, as well as from modern ideologies of power. And Christian theology finds its *relevance* in the hope for the *kingdom of the crucified one* in that it suffers with those who bear "the sufferings of this present time" (Rom. 8:18), and makes the cry of the oppressed its own cry, and fills it with hope of liberation and redemption. For the crucified one became the brother of the oppressed, the poor, and the abandoned, of those without legal rights, and of those who are unrighteous. Therefore brotherhood with these, the "least of his brethren," is a part of being a brother of Christ and not just an optional activity carried on by his church. Christian theology must be carried on among the people and with the people. It is contemporary theology only when it becomes a companion of those who suffer in the present time, as Paul says in Romans 8. There is therefore no "identity-involvement dilemma," for Christian identity with the crucified one means involvement in the suffering of the poor and the misery of the sorely oppressed. On the other hand, that involvement, when it is taken seriously, always means an identification with the crucified Christ. There is therefore no dilemma, but from the very first, the real and liberating tension of Christian faith.

Thesis 2. *Christian theology is being confronted today on various sides with false alternatives. In reality it has no alternative between evangelization and humanization, between interior conversion and improvement of conditions, or between the vertical dimension of faith and the horizontal dimension of love. Whoever separates and divides any of these, destroys the unity of God and man in the person and in the future of Christ.*

Many Christians and theologians today are no longer maintaining the real tension of the Christian faith and are fleeing toward one or the other side. In the World Student Christian Federation, meanwhile, this fruitful tension has led to a sharp polarization, which has had a paralyzing effect on many students.

There are student groups who understand themselves only as part of the political protest movement and thus have given up their Christian identity. They are thereby leaving the Bible and missionary initiative to politically conservative or unpolitically Christian groups. We see similar divisions occurring among theology students; pious students do not protest, and protesting students will no longer have anything to do with Christian piety. They are no longer bringing together the study of the Bible and the necessary political action. Nearly every denomination of Christianity is becoming polarized between those calling for old-fashioned soul-winning and those advocating new styles of social action that shock and startle the faithful. It is of crucial importance to theology that it overcome these false polarizations and senseless alternatives, and produce a unity in the tension.

Evangelization inevitably leads to involvement in the social and political problems of society. We begin by preaching the gospel, and then are faced with marriage and family problems, the problems of our children's upbringing and better education, of the organization of society, of work for the sick, the socially weak, and underprivileged. Evangelism is not only proclamation and personal calling but social action as well, and true evangelism has always been so.

On the other hand, it is not enough simply to improve the social and political conditions of man. Men must also be aroused out of their inner apathy and be encouraged to become self-reliant. Both works must be carried on at the same time, in a comprehensive approach that embraces the total field of human misery. To be sure, not everyone has to do both, but everyone should at least recognize the other charismata in the body of Christ.

"Transform yourselves," some say, "and then your conditions will change by themselves," and they join the evangelical movement. But unfortunately, conditions do not then cater to their wishes. Exploitation, capitalism, racism, and wars go on as ever. "Change conditions," others say, "and then men will also change," and they become socialists. But unfortunately, men do not then cater to their wishes. Marriage crises, suicide figures, and alcoholism mount as ever. We must therefore do both at the same time. Personal interior transformation without change in socio-economic conditions is an idealistic illusion—as if man were only a soul and not a body as well. Change in conditions without personal transformation of the inner man is a materialistic illusion —as if man were only a product of his conditions and nothing more. In the liberating practice of Christian faith, self-transformation and the changing of conditions coincide.

The real front line of the freedom of Christ does not lie between soul and body, individual and society, interiority and exteriority, but on the battlefield of the present in its totality, between the powers of the past—which Paul called sin, law, and death—and the forces of the future—which he called spirit, justice, and freedom. This front between the past and the future runs straight through every soul and every body, every person and every society. The interior experiences of the spirit in faith, assurance, and prayer are anticipations of the future of Christ's kingdom just as much as the breaking up of a ghetto, the cure of a sick person, a work of social justice or a successful revolution for liberation. It is not that a vertical dimension of faith stands in opposition to a horizontal dimension of political love, but that the future new creation struggles against the destructive forces of this passing world and of the existing societies. In Christ, God and the neighbor have become a unity; and what God joins together, let no man put asunder—least of all a theologian.

Thesis 3. *Christian theology must be biblical theology. In the Bible we encounter the remembrance of hope, which is both liberating and dangerous. The book of the promises of God is open toward the future of the kingdom of God. Biblical theolgy, therefore, must be neither historicist nor fundamentalist, but lead from the Bible to missionary and practical efforts for liberation. It is difficult to wage a revolution without the Bible (Ernst Bloch). It is even more difficult not to bring about a revolution with the Bible. (According to Acts 17:6: "These men who have turned the world upside down have come here also. . . .")*

Among new churches, the study of the Bible seems to stand in the foreground. That has its basis not only in missionary biblicism, but also in the surprises of a "love at first sight." In the old churches, Bible study and exegesis have passed into the background. There is greater preoccupation with philosophical theology, sociology of religion, and anthropology. That is unfortunately not based on the fact that the Bible is well-known—the Bible has, on the contrary, become quite unknown. It is based rather on a Christian tradition that leads men to expect nothing new from the Bible. Without biblical theology, however, theology cannot be Christian theology. We should do all we can, therefore, to stimulate theologians and Christians to study the Bible. That will, however, only be possible if we read the Bible with new perception, with new eyes.

In my opinion, the Bible is the book of the poor, the oppressed, and the hopeless. It is not the book of ruling priests and lords. It is also not a book of laws for the just, but of promises for the hopeless and of the gospel of God for sinners. In order to read this book properly, therefore, we must read it with the eyes, and in the community, of the poor, the godless, and the unjust. Then we read in it God's history with his enslaved and obstinate people of Israel as well as God's history with the crucified Jesus of Nazareth. In these accounts of the past we encounter the promissory history of the future of God. We find the future in the past, see the future revealed and anticipated in the past, and find ourselves taken up into this history of liberation.

Historicizing interpretation robs the Bible of the future that it promises. Fundamentalist interpretation deprives the Bible of its character as history. The book of the promises of God is open to the future, for all promises are striving for their fulfillment in the future. Every text in the Bible narrates the past in order to announce the future. We need not only to demythologize the Bible, but even more to "dehistoricize" it in order to free it from the chains of the past and to discover in it the future of God, which will become our future. And if we read it with the eyes of our own poverty and lowliness, we shall also "detheocratize" the Bible; for we shall find in it not the revelation of a God who rules and governs from above, but the God who suffers here below in his suffering people and who finally in his own suffering in his powerless Christ frees men from their domination and hubris.

Biblical theology says, "It is written," and means by that the promises of God. Ontology says, "It has happened," and means thereby reality that can be experienced. Someday there will really

come, out of the written word of the promise, the new reality of fulfillment. One day we shall see. One day we shall no longer encounter trial and contradiction in nature, history, and political life, but
shall arrive at harmony with them. But as long as we do not see
that day, so long as all tears have not been wiped away, we
should hold on to what is written, namely, the promise. We should
place greater value on the hope of our faith than on our visible
experiences and thus refuse to come to terms with any kind of
status quo (Hans Joachim Iwand).

I am not advocating a naive biblicism. If we read the Bible with
the eyes of the suffering, we shall see in it the hopes of God. Then
we shall realize that the Bible is a most revolutionary and even
subversive book. It does not have its time behind it two thousand
years ago, but rather ahead of it, because it points even beyond
our present time into the future of God. There are few memories
that are more liberating from the chains of the present and more
dangerous for the powerful of today than the biblical recollections
of hope. It was not without design that the reading of the Bible
was forbidden to the simple folk by pagan lords and a lordly
Christian church. Have such prohibitions perhaps become unnec-
cessary today because the church and theology have done their
best to render the Bible harmless?

Thesis 4. *Christian theology is eschatologically oriented theology. It thinks within the creative tension between the old and
the new, law and freedom, the letter and the spirit. Its general
field of operation is constituted by the expectations and apprehen-
sions of the future which mobilize or cripple people in history.*

If it is correct to say that the Bible is essentially a witness to the
promissory history of God, then the role of Christian theology is
to bring these remembrances of the future to bear on the hopes
and anxieties of the present. It must answer for the hopes which
are in Christians (1 Pet. 3:15). To do this, it must interpret the
promissory history in various ways. It must, first of all, discover
exegetically what the text meant literally, i.e., for the people of
biblical times. It must, secondly, determine what that means today
for our experiences, our actions, and our hopes. We call this
process of understanding and interpretation "hermeneutic." It
includes: (1) historical exegesis, which determines the literary

sense of a text or of a symbol; (2) the interpretation of the practical meaning of a text or of a symbol as it relates to the solution of our current life-problems; (3) an exposition of the meaning of our experience, for words and symbols without experience are empty; and, finally, (4) the presentation of the eschatological meaning of a text for that hope that drives men on to new actions and to new experiences. Hermeneutic unites, therefore, historical exegesis with present experience and hope in what is coming. It builds a bridge between past and future—that future for which the word spoken in the past sets the present free.

Here the specialization of theology creates a problem. Many theological faculties and seminaries have separated exegesis from historical studies and systematic from practical theology, thus obscuring the unity of theology. This unity should be demonstrated by interdisciplinary seminars. Otherwise students will no longer see the woods for the trees.

Christian theology thinks in creative antitheses. Its orientation toward the future of God makes it dialectic. The Bible itself is not a perfectly uniform book of revelation, but rather contains the antithesis between the Old and the New Testaments. Christian faith therefore arises out of tension, and it endures in the midst of a continuing conflict between the old and the new. How can Christian faith take its rise from such a conflict without thereby arriving at a consciousness of history that seeks again and again the "new" and overcomes the "old"? On nearly every page of the New Testament, we meet the key-word *new*: the new covenant, new tongues, the new commandment, a new name, new wine, a new creature, a new heaven, and a new earth, and finally the God whose last word is: "Behold, I make all things new."

The experience of this tension between the old that passes and the new that comes has also left its stamp upon the language of the Bible, as well as upon the languages into which the Bible has been translated. Conformably with this experience, the Hebrew language has no real form of the present; the essential elements in its conception of time are the past and the future. The faith of the Israelites is faith in a promise—and so is the Christian faith. The Christian lives for the future, which has already begun here and now.

There are many languages in the world which have no gram-
matical form for expressing future time. When Varro wrote the
first Latin grammar, he simply forgot the future tense. Indian
and African languages often have no genuine form of the future.
In these languages, "yesterday" and "tomorrow" can be inter-
changed, and words for time can even be used to designate space.
The language forms for expressing a consideration of the future
do not exist.

This leaves time linguistically without expectations, plans, or
goals. The "future" seems to be something indefinitely distant.
It is then easy to entertain the doctrine of a millennium which
has absolutely no effect upon the present. Not so with Pauline
eschatology, according to which the future of Christ already takes
hold and determines the present. For example, in the so-called
messianic churches in Africa the future has already dawned in
the presence of the Messiah. They thereby experience a present
filled with undreamed joy and an unusual release of energy.[1] Here
is a starting point for us to learn the new language of hope and
future.

Wherever people are so unaware of history that the antithesis
between the old and the new is not understood, Paul's antithesis
between law and freedom cannot be understood either. The law
remains in effect; the Old Testament dominates the New and is
interpreted according to legal principles. Christianity becomes
moralistic, legalistic, and rigoristic. The law of Israel and of one's
own people is expected to give that inner strength which only
faith in Christ, which liberates people from the law and its works,
can give them. Then the present has the past for its lord instead
of being governed by the future. Then a person is a Christian
insofar as certain moral restrictions are placed upon his behavior.
But what a Christian should do positively, no one any longer knows.

If Christian theology is to speak about God, freedom, and the
future, then it must make use of the thought contained in these
antitheses and discover linguistic forms for the future. Even the
classical and Germanic languages had not developed a viable form
of the future tense. Only the "alphabetization" of the nations by
the Bible brought into existence the language of history, of liberation, and of the future.

Thesis 5. *Christian theology will in the future become more and more a practical and political theology. It will no longer be simply a theology for priests and pastors, but also a theology for the laity in their callings in the world. It will be directed not only toward divine service in the church, but also toward divine service in the everyday life of the world. Its practical implementation will include preaching and worship, pastoral duties, and Christian community, but also socialization, democratization, education toward self-reliance and political life.*

Until now, most churches have developed theology in their seminaries. Theology was studied in a professional school for preachers. But theologians were thereby separated from the members of their communities— the educated from the uneducated as Greeks from Barbarians (cf. Rom. 1:14). The more people begin to "grow up" in our communities today, the more we shall need a theology for the layman who has "come of age," and for theologians who can answer his critical questions as well as listen to the layman's answers. In many Western countries today, seminaries are becoming empty, wherever they are not integrated into universities. Courses in departments of religion in the universities are surprisingly well attended, and indeed by students who are interested in theology and religion, but do not want to become clergymen. I believe this is a good development. First of all, it removes the distinction between clergy and laity; and secondly, the church must finally accept the fact that its theologians do not have to be sent into the world before anything can happen: its laity are already in the world.

Pastoral theology remains a part of theological formation, but it must be integrated into the wider horizon of the theological formation of the whole of Christianity, which is at work in very different practical spheres of society. This theology for the whole of Christianity "come of age" is only in its initial phases. Lay persons should not be trained to become "mini-pastors" who can relieve the pastor of his work. They should rather be trained to become men and women who can think independently and act in a Christian way in their own vocations in the world. It seems to me, therefore, meaningful to choose the expression *political theology* for this wider theology of Christianity in the world, for the *res publica* is of concern to all citizens. Man is a *zoon politikon* (political animal). The kingdom of God is to be anticipated in politics, not in a separate sphere, called religion. This new form of theology, namely, the political, will, in my opinion, enable us to bridge two gaps—the one inside the church which divides the clergy from the laity and the one outside which divides the church from the world. In the practical order, this means: first, the integration of church seminaries into universities, wherever this is possible; secondly, the building of our own Christian or free universities, wherever the first practice is not possible; and thirdly, the gathering of theologians in Christian centers for the education of the laity.

Thesis 6. *Christian theology is fundamentally a theology of dialogue. It has and reveals its truth first of all in dialogue with other people and other religions and ideologies. Its center lies on their boundaries. Its object is universal, and exists for all men. But because it can itself only be particular, it must discover and spread the universal truth in dialogue with others.*

The church is not universal, although it must be open for every man. Only God is universal. Christians are not already the true men, but Christ is the new man for them and all others. Out of this tension between the universality of truth and the particularity of its representation by men arises the necessity for Christian theology to be tolerant and ready for dialogue. It is in trusting in the absolute truth of God that theology can perceive its relative truth, and try to have discussion with others. Only those will refuse to have dialogue with Buddhists and Marxists who are afraid thereby of losing their faith, or who want to stamp out the truths of Buddhism and Marxism. I have myself taken part in the Christian-Marxist dialogue in Europe, and I found that it did not lead to an impoverishment but to an enrichment on both sides. We did not reproach each other for the mistakes of the past, but accepted each other seriously for our strong points. Christians and Marxists revealed themselves in this dialogue in a way unknown until then, and gave up their prejudices. "If we do not talk to each other, someday we will be shooting at each other." This is simply a fact. Dialogue is the only method of making and keeping peace, and only a dialogical church can be a church of peace.

Dialogue between the world religions and the ideologies of the modern world is necessary for the survival of mankind. Theology should strive to have dialogue everywhere, and the churches should create the conditions for it. This can be done in societies which are mixed religiously, ideologically, racially, and culturally, while it is very difficult in homogeneous societies or those based on apartheid. A theology that encapsulates itself in its own tradition and its own circles petrifies and dies. Christian theology needs to have dialogue for the sake of its own cause. Its partners need dialogue with Christian theology. We should create centers for dialogue, promote literature for dialogue, and call upon students to study other religions and modern sciences. The Christian faith will not thereby be relativized but rather be brought into relationships. A theology without relationships is a dead theology.

Theology should talk about the God who frees all men, and lays claim to them, so that they may live and not perish. The theologian is however only a man among other men. He will therefore combine his certainty in God with humility in his humanity, and thus esteem the truth that is greater than himself and his best theology. He will forget that *pride* which many earlier theologians used to display. He will, however, also overcome that *self-hatred* that modern theologians often manifest. Theology is a gratifying as well as a very humbling science. Only those who are honest about their human frailty can speak for it. This virtue, too, belongs to the formation of the theologian.

In the Old Testament there is a story about a theologian who is trying to find out who he is. It is the story of Jacob and his struggle with the angel of God at the Jabbok ford. Jacob wrestled with this angel the whole night, and at the break of day in his misery he gasped, "I will not let you go unless you bless me." Jacob came out of this wrestling with God a blessed man, that is, at the same time, a smitten man with a "disjointed hip." A good theologian is a man overcome by God. He speaks of God haltingly and takes no credit for himself.

> How small is that with which we wrestle,
> How great is that which wrestles with us,

said the poet Rilke.

This is the thing to notice about a theologian. As one who is conquered he nevertheless publishes hope in God's victory. Through his defeat he proclaims joy in God in the face of the enemies of human life.

NOTE TO CHAPTER ONE

1. J. Mbiti, "African Concept of Time," *African Theological Journal*, 1 (1968): 8–20; and Th. Sundermeier, "Gesetzund Gesetzlichkeit in den afrikanischen Kirchen," *Evangelische Theologie*, 31 (1971): 99 ff.

II.

"Where There Is Hope,
There Is Religion"

I. MYTHS OF HOPE

"Where there is hope, there is religion," says Ernst Bloch. He makes, however, an important addendum: "Where there is religion, there is not always hope." In this way he has made us aware of the world religions' ambivalent relationship to hope. The infinite hopes of man are preserved in the religions; but, by the same token, they are also abolished, betrayed, and rendered ineffective by the religions. Can hope become a key for understanding the world religions and indeed man's religious yearning itself? Can hope become the measure of our criticism of the religious illusions spawned by nations and people?

In the nineteenth century liberal as well as socialist philosophers tried to work out an *anthropology of religion*. "Religion is the sigh of the oppressed creature," announced Feuerbach and Marx. "Religion is a collective obsession," maintained Sigmund Freud. Under these presuppositions man comes to himself, his freedom, and his ego-intensity only when he gives up his religious projections and illusions and devotes himself exclusively to his earthly reality. The criticism of religion, without doubt, made modern man enlightened and clearheaded, but also poorer. He took up the task before him with sobriety and realism. Becoming a realist, however, meant not only losing all distance to his work, but also accommodating himself to his industrial society. Like Prometheus in charge of his own world, he set about the business of the day without the help of the gods. But in the upshot he is more like Sisyphus, suffering a coerced labor with which he saddled himself, in a prison which he himself built.

In this essay we want to inquire about an *eschatology of religion*. Our purpose is to reproduce, from the religious traditions, forms and symbols of that hope which does not impoverish but enriches man. We are inquiring about a hope which does not deceive or limit man in his freedom but opens up for him new horizons of his future. We are asking about a hope which can incite man for the future, embolden him for freedom, and inflame him for the possible, thereby subduing his depression and melancholy over the present state of his life and his society. We would like to overcome Sisyphus and his absurd world. We would like to search out the way of Abraham who left his land, his family, and his house to seek the promised land through the power of hope.

Where, then, is hope preserved in the religions?

Greek mythology speaks of hope in the legend of Prometheus. Through the rear door, behind the back of Zeus, the father of everything, Prometheus slunk into Olympus, lit a torch from the sun's fiery car, and stealthily made his way back to earth—undetected. Through Prometheus' theft from the divine quarters, mankind was gifted with fire. When Zeus realized this, he swore revenge. He made a woman, Pandora, the most beautiful ever fashioned, and sent her to Epimetheus, the brother of Prometheus. This fellow wasted no time in marrying her, but she was just as dumb as she was beautiful. She opened the box of Prometheus even though it was forbidden her. And out of the box came everything evil which from that time on has plagued mankind: sickness, insanity, vices, and, the worst of all, hope. For deceitful hope, which Prometheus had also locked up in the box, restrained men plagued by these evils from putting an end to their suffering through freely willed death (Hesiod).

Hope is, therefore, according to this myth, an evil out of Pandora's box. In addition to all other evils, man acquired yet another: hope. It deceives him with illusions and thus intensifies all his sufferings. If we were able to be free of hope, then we would be able to come to terms with all forms of our suffering. We would no longer experience our suffering as pain. We would then have no more fear; without fear and without hope we would be invulnerable like the Stoics. Hope is a fraud. Only if one sees through this deception is he or she at peace. Give up hope, then you are happy!

Mircea Eliade has shown us how closely fear and hope belong

together and how both are provoked by the "horrors of history." The "horrors of history" lie in the accidental, incalculable, sinister, and hidden future. The "horror of history" is identical with the "horror of the future," to which archaic man is helplessly handed over. History is chaos, and future is change, transformation, and destruction. Hence ancient man always took a negative attitude toward the events of history. There was no divine meaning in them. Consequently, in his culture he built an order (*kosmos*) against the wild chaos of nature and at the center of his culture erected the cultic place (temple) where gods lived. Likewise, his religious festivals celebrated a yearly recurring order against chaotic, transient time. Life degenerates in time, but the origin of life is repeated in the great festivals. In the Babylonian new year's festival, the time of the past year is reborn. The cosmogony is repeated and people can begin again with the origin of the world. The smaller weekly festivals were also occasions in which elaborated time could become new again.

The Greek philosophers also reflected on a periodical renewal of the world (*metakosmesis*) out of its incessantly repetitious descent into chaos and into passing time. What therefore is history? It is the way, constrained by destiny, into what is alien. What is salvation? It is the homecoming to the lost paradise, the return to the origin. Mircea Eliade has called this the "myth of the eternal return." In the incessant repetition of each moment and event of the cosmos, the impression of its transiency shows itself to be mere appearance (*doxa*). In its ground, its essence or its origin everything remains in its place. Historic becoming and passing away is only an appearance, for in the ground of being the archetypes or the ideas of the external *logos* rule.

Religions intend to expel "the horrors of history" by means of these figures and symbols of the "eternal return of the same" which serve to abolish history or make it unconscious. They stabilize the flux of becoming. In the experienced horrors of history, it is not hope in a better future which is saving but the memory of a sacred origin.

With this in mind, we could quite easily have the impression that where religion is, hope not only does not reign but is actually banished. Yet this impression is misleading. Myth and utopia,

memory and hope always exist in close proximity. The myth of
the sacred origin in paradise and the myth of the eternal return
are both utopian counterschemes to chaos and passing time. They
are utopias of order which provide man, who is delivered over to
history, with a stabilizing counterscheme, a counterenvironment to
his daily struggle. Because real life is subjected to the horrors of
history, only the counterworld of the mythical, heavenly, or eternal
order offers man balance and the chance of survival. These religious myths can be called daydreams of people in which the
anxieties of the night are vanquished. And if these myths all speak
of a primal sacred life when men once lived together in intimacy
with the gods, it is also true that their hope is expressed in this
memory. They are dreams turned backward or hopes in the mode
of the memory of pure being. To be sure, one did not hope that
out of the horrors of history and of the dark future something
new or ultimately good would proceed, but rather that the return
to the origin and the return of the same would vanquish the horrors of history. But even this is a form of hoping confidence in
being and a utopia of the highest rank.

In a certain distinction from other peoples and religions Israel,
because of its peculiar encounter with God, experienced and lived
its own life and viewed the life of the whole world as history open
to the future. At its origin there does not stand a mythical primal
event, as in Babylon and Egypt. but an historical event: the rebellion and exodus from slavery in Egypt. Israel experienced its "God
of the fathers" in this event as a God of promise, a God of hope, as
the exodus God. It experienced itself as a people who had been
set on the way from the past into the future. It understood this
exodus event not as a mythical event of the origin but as an historic
event which pointed beyond itself to a greater future of God. In
Greek and Oriental mythology, the past is made present as a
perpetual origin; according to the Israelite view, however, the past
is a promise of the future. The God of the future sets himself
against the gods of the origin. We see this clearly in the harsh
religious confrontation between Yahweh and the baalim in Canaan
and finally in the clearest possible terms in the prophets.

The Israelite religion, from its inception on, had a messianic
tendency. Saving power against the horrors of history, of which

Israel's own history was full, was not identifiable with a mythic utopia of the primal order or the pure being behind this evil world of appearance or the eternal return of the same. Saving power was rather to be found in the confidence of hope in the coming God. Out of the dark future, the Israelites heard the summoning voice of the promising God whose glory is to fill all lands at the end. Here religion was not claimed against the horrors of history, but, quite to the contrary, was understood as an eschatological picture of the future which is to be realized through history and the God of history. Hope in the coming God affords possibilities of accepting historic suffering and of recognizing historic tasks, yet without being annihilated. Comparable to the compass's function of giving us orientation in the earth's space, this hope gives us orientation in time by pointing in a constant direction to the kingdom of God as the goal and fulfillment of history. This hope does not take up the gods' claim of being against meaningless history, but takes up the claim of the God of history for the future of this history. With this, history itself also loses something of its mere horrors. It is not simply transiency, chaos, and destruction which now constitute history, but also the possibilities of the new which this God creates.

If in connection with religious myths we have spoken of *utopias of order* against the experience of chaos, we can in connection with the messianism of the Israelite religion, speak of the *utopias of freedom* for the experience of the new and the ultimately new in history. Hope makes its exit from the constraint of the "eternal return of the same" and is, so to speak, "curious" about the future. It opens up men for pain in the suffering of history and opens them up still more for that grace which is "new every morning" and thus at the end "will make everything new."

Indeed with Israel the religion of hope comes toward us out of the world of religions. There is in it a criticism of the mythical religions. Yahweh is not baal. The exodus God is not the idol of a nation or of a given reality. But there is also in it a liberation of that yearning and hope which in the other religions are traced by the mythical counterschemes to the horrors of history. Where there is hope, there is, therefore, religion as well as criticism of religion.

II. A HUMAN BEING IS A CREATURE OF HOPE

If we want to verify this religion of hope, we must outline an anthropology of hope as well as an ontology of the not-yet.

For a long time, hope has been counted among the affects and moods of humans and described only in psychological terms. Therefore its exchange rate has quite often fluctuated with the times. Spinoza thought that hope was always bound up with fear and that fear and hope betray the weakness of our souls. For many others, hope was an opium for people who would like to escape reality and hence the most infantile form of the illusion principle. According to Freud, one can be freed from the illusion principle only by the reality principle.

Today we understand hope quite differently. Dostoevsky wrote: "The ant knows the formula of his ant hill. The bee knows the formula of his beehive. They do not know their formula in a human way, but in their own way. And they don't need to know more. Only man does not know his formula." With this epigram he wanted to say that man is not a finished creature like an ant or a bee. His essence is not handed to him as a finished product but assigned to him as a task. Thus he is hidden to himself and constantly in search of his true essence. He is for himself and for his equals an open question, a puzzle, and often a dread. He must himself give the answer to humanity, and yet in history he can consider none of his answers as final. Man in his mere existence is an experiment. It can be attributed to his messianic nature that he must go to the boundaries of his possibilities and even beyond them in order to find himself.

Hoping does not mean to *have* a number of hopes at one's disposal. It means, rather, hoping to *be* open. Despair does not mean to bury a few hopes here or to destroy a few illusions there, but to give up one's openness and thus oneself. To be in hope (*Hoffend-Sein*) means to find oneself in a state of preparedness, not to commit oneself to what has passed by and not to tie oneself to wish-dreams, but to harmonize with the experiment which one himself is. In this sense, hope is not something which one man has and the other does not have, but is a primal mode of existing or the most important constituent of human life. Man hopes as long as he lives and, conversely, he lives in the liveliness peculiar to him as long as he hopes.

The behavioral sciences have shown how every animal has its own kind of environment which belongs to it as the necessary externality of the internal side of its instincts. Birds need air in order to fly. Fish need water in order to swim, etc. But man, so say some, is not bound to a definite environment. He is a world-open creature who himself can and must everywhere build his own environment in his cultures. And yet there is an element and an environment without which he cannot live as man, and that is hope. It is the breath of life.

Therefore, we mean here by hope (1) a peculiar kind of specific human openness and (2) that medium, element, and atmosphere for the specific human being.

If on this basis we call man a "creature of hope," we are reaching beyond the other anthropologies which call man the logos-defined animal (*zoon logon echon*) or the political animal (*zoon politicon*) or the tool-making animal. For all of these definitions relate to the environment which man must create culturally, but not to his open historicity which places man in his innermost existence on the threshold between the vanishing today and the ever newly appearing tomorrow. In hope, we understand that man knows no definitive experiences but constantly recognizes new oppositions, impulses, and opportunities and in this way shows his liveliness. He is a discoverer, a conqueror, a producer of symbols and works, a player, but always a creature who sees himself, as it were, over his shoulder and looks beyond the present into the future. Indeed, there is no expression of life without the unconscious or conscious entrance of an intended future.

It has always been difficult to define the essence of human existence. In the history of his culture, man has ever and again a new face. Because he is not essentially determined, he is like an actor who can appear in countless different roles. But it is nevertheless possible to designate the direction in which man is heading. The essence of man consists in a perspective and expectation rather than in a definable and fixed appearance. In hope, man recognizes every situation in which he finds himself as a station on the way, which he must pass beyond and leave behind in order to

realize his humanity. This direction rules not only his spirit but
also his body. We are able to diagnose it in the lines of his spirit
as well as of his body, for in this directedness he suffers and acts
always as a total and integral being. If man loses this direction of
his total behavior, he becomes sick; then his conduct becomes
retrogressive. He is afflicted with anachronism. Men die when
they are suddenly struck with the impression that everything is
without prospect for them. They simply give up even if there are
no physical causes for their death. Others become criminals out of
hopelessness. A young burglar in Berlin related that he had sought
a job at different places, but was again and again thrown out. "And
then came the point where nothing made any difference to me."
This is typical. He became a criminal because his hope in life had
turned into self-hate and he had given up on himself. Both,
death from expired hope and criminality from hopelessness, show
that man, as a temporal creature, is directed toward the future and
that this is a direction which alone corresponds to hope. In distinction from an animal, man can fail himself; and to be sure, not
only in individual acts. He can fail himself totally. His hope is
therefore simultaneously the epitome of the life-risk which he
must take up. He can win himself; he can lose himself; in any
case, he himself is at stake.

Since the beginning of the Enlightenment, there has been a sustained endeavor to rationalize man's fantasy-filled connection with
the world. Everywhere men have traveled the way from myths and
utopias to science. We think rationally and causally, and view
what is not included in this form of intellectual penetration as
epiphenomena or mirages without particular significance for the
forces which really move the world. What does not offer itself as
rationally explicable, be it causal or intentional, is likewise not
considered to be real. Fantasy is considered a more primitive intellectual process, for it disregards the reality principle (Alexander
Mitscherlich). Yet of all the sayings which decorated the walls of
the Sorbonne in Paris in May, 1968, one attracted particular attention far beyond France. It demanded: *"L'imagination au pouvoir!"*
"Power to imagination!"

But what is fantasy? Even Immanuel Kant, who condemned all
metaphysical speculations as "dreams of a visionary" and in his

Critique of Pure Reason reduced reason to the limits of possible experience, spoke of a transcendental imagination. Romantics such as Novalis and Schleiermacher extolled fantasy as practical reason because it makes present what is still absent, visualizes the ideal, and places the spirit in that freedom which carries it far beyond every authority and limitation. They praised fantasy as the imagination of hope against that flat rationalism for which only what is and what can be calculated is rational. But with what does the fantasy of man occupy itself, and how does it do it?

In his analyses of dreams, Sigmund Freud studied pathological cases. In his reproductive fantasy, man is occupied with experiences which he could not master but had to repress. In his dreams the repressed past shows up again in his consciousness and he is forced to come to terms with his experiences. Thus repressed guilt, for example, appears in his dreams. Suppressed impulses seek their liberation in dreams. This reproductive fantasy, which works on the unmastered past, occurs especially in the night dreams of man.

It is obviously quite another matter with daydreams. Indeed not only sick people have dreams. The healthy and happy also have dreams. It is not only unpleasant experiences which dreams evoke but also peak experiences. In these daydreams, a "not-yet-conscious" demonstrates itself, that is, an anticipation of the future which is not yet in existence. This fantasy, which shows itself on the threshold of the present which we know and the future which we do not know, can be called productive fantasy. It is a fantasy which is fascinated by the possible new. It is a poetic imagination which does not wish to change the unbearable past but to anticipate the still unrealized future in order to anticipate and shape it in thought and pictures. The liberating power of this productive fantasy has been scarcely recognized and celebrated, yet it is effective wherever people live and hope. The so-called realists have defamed it as mere wishful thinking. They have maintained that it is only an illusory means by which unliberated and passive people take their flight into the future.

But this defamation is simply false. In his night dreams man is forced to come to terms with his repressed past. He needs this work of grief to be able to live. The most striking thing about modern

man's mentality is his inability to mourn. But in his daydreams he
is free, to some extent, for the anticipation of his future. He needs
these anticipations in order not to fall backward into the future.
"The god of physics gives us what we wish. But he does not tell us
what we should wish," Santayana once said. The calculating
understanding fulfills our wishes. It explains to us how we can
rule over things, but it says nothing about what we should do
with the mastered forces of nature. Only the productive fantasy
of reason can formulate meaningful wishes. In view of the hyper-
trophy of the technical intellect, we are in a position to do much
of what we want. But today we simply no longer know what we
really want. Men have become gods of nature but unfortunately
not particularly imaginative and creative gods. Hence it is right:
"Power to imagination!" The sciences and futurology place at our
disposal numerous possible and planable futures. But do we have
any representations of a wishable future? Automation, cybernetics,
and futurology call out, so to speak, for the leading visions of the
productive fantasy, for a future in which we can hope. Human
reason must finally become creative again and we must put into
practice the sketches of a desirable future. After three hundred
years of rationalism's trend from utopia to science, the reverse
way from science to utopia, without giving up science, owns priority on today's agenda. In this way can we make theoretical reason
serviceable to practical reason.

The productive fantasy always works with wishful thinking. It
goes beyond the reality principle. It must do this because it reaches
into the dimensions of the possible in order to select out of it what
should be realized and rejects those possibilities which should not
be realized. It also works with projections and illusions. Against
Feuerbach and his criticism of religion, one must say that projections are in no way merely compensations for disappointed and
suffered reality. Rather, they are stimulated by objective new possibilities. They are projections into a possible but yet unknown
future. Against Freud, one must maintain that illusions are in
no way merely mental gratifications of repressed wishes but—as the
word *illusion* means in its Latin origin—preludes, overtures to
the future, a mental form coordinating and presenting itself in
representations of the not-yet-realized future.

III. THE WORLD IS A "LAND OF UNLIMITED POSSIBILITIES"

An anthropology of hope would hang in the air if the reality of the world in which we live were in itself a closed system. "Nothing new happens under the sun," said Koheleth. But if nothing new can happen in the world, then there is also no real future. If there is no future, then there is also no meaningful history. If there is no history, then the world is not open ahead, but is closed in itself. Then man cannot be a hoping and free creature but is imprisoned in himself and is only a small wheel in the enormous world machinery. Therefore, to an anthropology of hope there necessarily belongs an ontology of the future open world, i.e., of history.

It is the greatness of Ernst Bloch, whom we are basically following here, that he has developed not only a "principle of hope" for man, but also an ontology of the not-yet-being and of possibility in the world process. Without real chances, the hope of man is meaningless. With this notion, Bloch—perhaps in a degree greater than he himself was aware—could have a close connection with American philosophy. In a lecture which he gave on the hundredth birthday of William James in 1942 in Cambridge (Mass.), he quoted James: "Realities swim in an extensive sea of possibilities out of which they are selected." In Bloch's own book on the ontology of the not-yet-being (1961), the same image is found with almost the same formulation: "The already real is surrounded by a sea of possibilities and again and again a new piece of reality arises out of this sea." Whereas for James man selects from the sea of possibilities that which is to be realized, for Bloch the sea of possibilities is itself productive of the realities which rise out of it like islands. This is the difference. But common to both is the fact that they value the category of possibility higher than the category of reality. From Romantic philosophy until the present (Nicholai Hartmann, Martin Heidegger), we find the ontological principle: "Higher than reality stands possibility," even if before Bloch there was scarcely any inquiry into the different categories of possibility. If we understand reality as the realization of possibility, then this necessitates an ontology of that which is not yet but is possible or stands in possibility. Thus to man's mode of reality there logically belongs a mode of possibility. We find it in the productive fantasy of hope, for hope, according to Kierkegaard, is the "passion for the possible."

But there are different kinds of possibility: there are real possibilities and unreal possibilities. Correspondingly, there are world-transforming and world-denying hopes as well as concrete utopias and abstract utopias. It is not easy, however, to find out which possibilities are real and which unreal. There are utopias that play with possibilities that in their time are unreal but in later time can become quite real, as, for example, the ancient utopia of travel to the moon. We can never forgo setting up goals which are not attainable at the moment, for such goals give the present possible transformation a far-reaching sense. What is now impossible can only become possible if it is announced in a time in which it is still considered impossible (Leszek Kolakowski). But if the world in which we live and hope presents a mixture of realities and possibilities, then we may not see it as a finished house of being but as an open process. Then the world becomes not a system with eternally repeatable structures, but an open history in which something new happens and can be realized. Then it is not a completed creation but an open creative process and the world is in itself a great experiment, a *laboratorium possibilis salutis* (a laboratory of possible salvation), as Bloch says. It is not a heaven of fulfillment; neither is it a hell of annihilation. Rather it is an unfinished earth. In its possibilities it is open for good and for evil. Its future can be the universal death, the nothing *(nihil)*, or the home of identity, the all. The world process is still undecided. Thus like the old apocalypsts, Bloch maintains "the true genesis is not at the beginning but at the end. Man still lives everywhere in prehistory, indeed each and everything still stands before the creation of the world as a right world."

Where is this open world process decided? For Bloch it is decided by the bravery of hope on the front line of the present. Bloch, therefore, searches for a "corps of the anti-nothing" which on the basis of its hope in life does not abandon this world to evil, the inhuman, and the powers of death. In the midst of wars and the many repressions of better human possibilities, this corps of the anti-nothing remains faithful to the dream of salvation. This is for Bloch the resurrection's point of hope: death swallowed up in the victory of life. But for him this fixed point of hope is sustained exclusively by the human will in its dawn. There is no guarantee. Hope becomes practical if it grasps today the real possibilities in order to repel the spheres of the negative, of evil and suffering. In league with the real possibilities which are at hand in the world, hope must become militant and take sides with life against death, peace against war, and the poor and oppressed against their oppressors.

To be sure, Bloch's philosophy is atheistic. But it is also thoroughly religious. Without the memory of that religion of hope from the Old and New Testaments, there would be for him also no unequivocality. For man is an ambiguous creature, open to good and evil. He always stands between hope and anxiety. The world is also ambiguous. New life, of course, is continually coming into the world, but every living thing must also die. Nature is the mother of all living creatures but at the same time Moloch-like, devouring her own children. Unequivocality in hope and in the will to life arises only when we go beyond man and the world. This happens in religious experience.

In religious experience hope is turned around. Here we realize that God is not simply the point of our hope in heaven, but that we are his hope on earth. In such experiences man attains the unforgettable impression that he is, together with other people and this whole creation, the utopia of God. "God created all things with finality," says an old rabbinical commentary on the creation story, "but he created man in hope." With the experiment "man" and the experiment "world" God has joined a hope. That gives man an unambiguous certainty of hope precisely at the place and time when he can no longer see any future ahead of him. It simultaneously places him in the open question of how he wants to fulfill, personally and together with society, that hope which God has placed in him and this world.

IV.   RELIGION OF HOPE IN THE MODERN SOCIAL SYSTEM

Between the individual man and his hope and the open possibilities in the world process, there stands society, which today is increasingly a technocratic society built according to the model of the "closed system." There is arising around man an ever thickening and more impenetrable nexus of relationships, dependencies, orders, and systems. He lives in megalopolis, in ever greater economic entanglements. The political orders and systems are interwoven into one another. Man has to live in these impenetrable relationships. Yet within them it is becoming increasingly more difficult to maintain that hope of which we have spoken, for the feeling of impotency is much more intense. "Beyond atheism, this is really the situation alienating us from God: to have to live in enormous contexts which we can effectively integrate neither intellectually nor morally" (Arnold Gehlen). Therefore, we find that today those very hopes with which the technocratic society was built up are disintegrating.

Industrialization began with the chiliastic pathos that finally the human kingdom of man could now be built, a kingdom of eternal freedom, a kingdom of eternal peace, as Auguste Comte said. "Our technical capability is brimming with promises of a new freedom, extended human dignity, and unlimited striving," Emmanuel Mesthene still maintained in 1966 at the World Conference for Church and Society in Geneva.

But when people see how obstinately our white and capitalistic as well as socialistic societies hinder that human society which would by all means be possible, then others fall into an apocalyptic depression. They can no longer combine any hope with the work-world of their fathers, the boring suburb paradise of their mothers, and the passive television cult. They see only an apocalyptic destruction of the world coming. Therefore, one segment of these people flees into the better past and dreams of the golden years when law and order still reigned, when everyone still knew the station and rank to which he belonged in society, when Germany was still great and America was still good. We find these dreams of social romanticism—dreams of the golden age—among people in the provinces who no longer understand the modern world. They are the "silent majority" who tend toward the radicalism of the right (in Germany, the United States, England, and France), even if they are thereby promised only the fulfillment of the quasi-religious yearning for the origin.

Another segment of people suffering from apocalyptic depression flees into inner emigration: "Split the scene! Leave society!"

cry the Hippies with Hermann Hesse. "You must flee life's compulsion into the heart's quiet places. Freedom is only in dreams and the beautiful blooms only in song," say the cultured people in Germany with Schiller. They also have given up hope and draw themselves back into the snail-shells of their lives. But their children flee even further in inner revolt, transcendental meditation, or pot delirium.

Finally, the militant left and protesting youths rebel against a futureless, brutal society and seek the total revolution. "A completely new society must be built. We don't know what kind of new society. We will find out." For the most part, they protest and rebel not because they have a concrete utopia of hope in a better society, but out of disgust, boredom, and hatred for society and for themselves.

A society which offers people no chance to define their future for themselves becomes a closed society and an inwardly and outwardly oppressive society. Together with hope it kills humanity.

The present forms of chiliastic enthusiasm about the progress of technology, apocalyptic depression inside the technocratic society, romantic yearning for the past of the golden age, inner emigration, and militant protest can be comprehended as forms of ruined hope, despairing hope, hope without the power of patience.

The religions of hope, Christianity and Judaism, will have to find their action and draw up their lines of battle precisely here, where hope is threatened by despair. For the medium of Jewish and Christian faith is the messianic field of hopes and disappointments.

III.

Ernst Bloch and Hope without Faith

I. TOWARD A DIALOGUE WITH "ESOTERIC MARXISM"

I am concerned here with a variety of Marxist humanism which we encounter in so-called esoteric Marxism. Its beginnings can be distinguished in certain post–World War I writings, notably those of Ernst Bloch (*Spirit of Utopia*, 1918, 1923), Georg Lukács (*History and Class Consciousness*, 1923), and Karl Korsch (*Marxismus und Philosophie*, 1923); its findings were endorsed with the rediscovery and first publication in 1932 of the so-called Paris Manuscripts of the young Marx. Only Ernst Bloch remained true to the visions of his youth, visions which he developed and substantiated in his major work, *Das Prinzip Hoffnung*, written in the period 1938–1949 while he was in America as a refugee from Nazi Germany. Its publication in the German Democratic Republic (1954–1959; West German edition, 1959) resulted in his flight to the West.[1]

Esoteric Marxism is a movement within Marxism which goes far beyond the recognized limits of the Leninist and Stalinist systems. On the one hand, it returns to the pre-Marxist sources of prophetic history, to Judaism and Christianity, and to the religious and political manifestations of the history of revolution in the West; on the other hand, it posits a future which goes beyond the goal of a classless society. Bloch has called this movement the "warm stream" in Marxism.[2] It is the "radiation" (*warmes Rot*) received from an as yet unrealized future of man and the world. This radiation compels a permanent transcending of present conditions and achievements through an orientation toward the objects of hope which promise a "home of identity" for all who are now suffering, laboring, and open to the future. In the "radiation" an attempt is made to find the ultimate meaning of life.

The warm stream derives from an indestructible hope in a new

life, in a *novum ultimum,* in the moment of which one can say
with Goethe's Faust, "Stay, you are so beautiful"; or, in biblical
terms, in the "new heaven and the new earth." This warm stream
must be combined with scientific and critical social analysis, lest
it degenerate into enthusiastic impotency. It must never become
mere economic analysis, however, lest it betray its whole dialectical
purpose. Thus it appears in the form of critical and self-critical
Marxism and, within the structures of a society built on state
socialism, opposes the institutionalized Marxist ideology of a particular state (Leszev Kolakowski). It corresponds to the internal
changes in Western Marxism and, in opposition to the expanding
materialism of consumption in both East and West, continually
seeks dialogue with Christianity. In this respect, it feels particularly related to certain heterodoxies of Christian history such as
Montanus, Marcion, Joachim di Fiore, Thomas Münzer, and the
Russian messianists.

A common basis for dialogue with the esoteric form of Marxism
might be found in the following areas:

(1) Biblical prophecy and the historical prophecies of the Old
and New Testaments, particularly the apocalyptic form of both
Israel and Christianity insofar as they understand themselves as
religions of the exodus and of the kingdom of the resurrected
Christ. For as Bloch says: "The eschatological conscience came
into the world through the Bible."[3]

(2) The history of the church and of Christian heretics insofar
as it concerns the present significance of apocalyptic for criticism
of the church, of society, and of the state.

(3) The messianic interpretation of modern times as the dawn-
ing of the "new age" and the "new world."

In this esoteric form of Marxism, atheism is meaningful only
to the extent that it can help to liberate man to self-fulfillment
and aid him in his own formation of human history. It is directed
against the God hypostases which are understood as that which
unburdens man of freedom and activity. It is not directed, however, against the liberating content of the Bible's hopes, such as
the "kingdom of God" and the "resurrection of the dead." One
can therefore understand it as an atheism for the sake of God and
his kingdom.

In view of these common bases, the method of the dialogue cannot be a diastasis between Christianity and esoteric-Marxist hope in the realization of the future of modern times. On account of the Christian elements in this hope, Christianity must not have recourse to an (un-) holy alliance with the prevailing forces. On the other hand, it is not enough to concentrate on the appearance of detached and now latently effective manifestations of the Christian spirit in this form of Marxism. A mere demonstration of the Christian origins of modern secular forms says nothing at all about their future. In fact in this humanism we find a biblical *logos spermatikos*. Otherwise the dialogue would hardly be possible.

However, we must not limit the discussion to a listing of correspondences. It must become more than a way of inducing this *logos spermatikos* to return to the wholeness of the *logos* of the church. What it can and must do is to stimulate the *logos* of hope, for which Christians are held accountable, to seek out the way of giving up oneself in this world in order to gain the future of the kingdom. The biblical image of the grain of wheat which bears no fruit without dying in the fields of this world helps us to see that the dissemination, the diaspora, the investment of the Spirit in the openness of history for the sake of the coming kingdom is precisely the commission of Christianity. Indeed, Christian hope can learn much in regard to its own activation from this revolutionary humanism. Only in this way can this humanism then learn from its side that when its own residues of Christian hope are reduced to the practical possibilities, the expected future fulfillment of all human existence is still not yet achieved. A dialogue with this humanism which is seeking a "future without God" can become a suasion to Christians to cease seeking "God without his future." In such a dialogue the world-transforming aspect of Christian eschatology must be emphasized precisely so that the world-transcending aspect of Christian hope may be meaningfully communicated.

II.   THE PRINCIPLE OF HOPE AND CHRISTIAN HOPE

The conception of man as that being absolutely oriented toward the future occurs in various forms in modern philosophical anthropology. He is the "first born in creation" (Herder), the "not fully

defined animal" (Nietzsche), a being "not adequately equipped by
nature" and therefore in need of civilization (Arnold Gehlen), a
being of "excentric positionality" (Helmut Plessner), a "utopian
being" who has not yet found the authentic *topos* of his humanity
(Ortega y Gasset). The novel contribution of Ernst Bloch's philosophy is that he does not reduce this openness of man and his
hope to mere inwardness, postponing, as it were, his fulfillment
to a hereafter. Instead he aligns "man's openness to the world"
with an ontology of the world's openness to man. The openness of
man which is apparent in his hopes corresponds to the openness of
the world process which is apparent in its possibilities. "Reality
is process."[4] Everything real goes beyond its processual front into
the possible. Only the real-possible (*Real-Mögliche*) provides the
utopian imagination of man with its concrete correlative. Only if
the category of possibility—long underestimated by philosophers
—receives adequate attention can that process be understood in
which human hope is mediated with matter so that, in this process
of labor and mediation, the "new" of the future can be grasped
on the front line of the present.

A new conception of reality is required to change man's mere
subjective hope into "learned hope" (*docta spes*) and to activate
work in the context of the historical future of the world and man.
This concept of reality comprehends reality together with its possibilities and matter together with its future; it must prevail
against the late nineteenth-century nonpurposive positivism which
Engels introduced into Marxist materialism and with which he
negated its original dialectic and reliance on a process. Similarly,
it must stand up against a noncommital idealism of pure illusion.
If matter is considered historically by setting it in the categories of
"future," "*novum*," and "front line," then this historical and
dialectical materialism must also prevail against the mythical and
philosophical model of the circle, of the "eternal return of the
same," and subjectively of *anamnesis* (remembrance). "That hope,
which at any final point, is not satisfied to have reached only its
starting point, overcomes the mere cyclic movement."[5] Its end
point is a new point; its beginning finds meaning only in its end.

It is now clear how it is possible to draw notions from biblical
apocalytic in order to bring ultimate aims into dialectical ma-

terialism. These scriptural ideas, however, can be brought into the dialectical and historical process of the mediation of man and nature only if that which occurs without any mediation—the sudden and transcendent end as understood in the Bible—is translated into what is subject to mediation: immanent transcending without transcendence. Here the cosmological apocalyptic of biblical theology undergoes demythologization; it does not emerge without reductions. The divine creative impulse is now seen in the core of matter itself. The ever fruitful womb of matter brings forth the forms of being in continually new and rich abundance, and man is the highest realization of its fecundity. The forms and tendencies of history are born from a dialectical mediation of human hopes and the possibilities inherent in nature, of the core of man which is not yet processed out and of the still hidden subject of nature. Therefore, the eschatological goal is to be found in the "humanization of nature" and the "naturalization of man." But this goal as such is at stake in history; it may be thwarted or it may also succeed. Only the courage of hope decides whether "all" or "nothing" is the outcome.

The transcendence of the creator is made immanent in the creating matter. This demythologization is seen as necessary to the activation of human hope. In reality, the result is a remythologization of nature, which had already lost its divine mystification in Israel and Christianity insofar as it was understood as creation and as world of God. One must ask whether it is necessary to pay such a price for the activation of hope in the process of history.

The same problem occurs again if one asks about the place of the negative in the dialectical process of real possibility and hope,[6] for the subjection of the negative in the progressing negation of the negative is conceived as the power of the dialectic. It grasps the negative in the counter move of being. Nothingness as such, however, is never entirely identical with the negation that has been drawn into the process. In this dialectical process, nothingness itself—"the enormous power of the negative" (Hegel)—is ontologized into "not-yet." Only as not-yet-being can it be informed with future new being. In not-yet-being, active hope can attain to something productive. To the extent to which hope is attached to objective possibility, "the fields where the negative is nothing but crisis unto death decrease."[7] "Active hope moves in not-having and rejoices in becoming; it has taken an oath of loyalty to the land which is known at least as anti-nothingness."[8] However true this may be for active hope in the open possibility of history it means that hope is reduced to pragmatology. Only in this sense does it become "learned hope." It must ignore the regions over which nothingness holds sway and where human beings experience suffering and death. Active hope has learned nothing about suffering. The "ontology of not-yet-being" comprehends nothingness only to the extent that courageous hope can accomplish something and has to leave no-longer- being in suffering and death without hope. "The power of the spirit is only as great as its pouring out, its depth only as deep as it dares to extend and to lose itself in its self-expression," said Hegel.

The biblical stories speak of the spirit of hope which is placed in God, and which, therefore, even in the midst of nothingness, puts its trust in the power of the *creator ex nihilo*. Being is called into life *ex nihilo* and not from the primal urge of matter. God's creative act takes place in that which is without form and void and in the darkness over the abyss. The Spirit of the Lord brings Ezekiel the promise of life as he stands in the valley of death (Ezekiel 37). The creative power of God is seen in Isaac's sacrifice, in the abandonment of Job, in Christ crucified, in nothingness, and in the total annihilation of all hope. What is in the beginning *creatio ex nihilo* is in the end *novum ex nihilo*, "life from the dead" (Rom. 11:15). In this way God is proclaimed here. Even where the force of the negative puts an end to all possibilities of man and nature, trust is placed in God, for God is the power of a future which proves itself creative over against total nothingness. This power is not identical with the power of present reality or of the future's open possibility. It is believed and hoped in at that precise point where people come face to face with the negative. The gravity of the negative and the deadliness of death need not be made harmless in order to activate the world-transforming power of Christian hope. If Christian hope derives from trust in the God "who gives life to the dead and calls into existence the things that do not exist" (Rom. 4:17), it has confidence enough to wage open war against the negative forces according to the possibilities which open it up. For the dogmatic restraint of hopelessness, *ex nihlo nihil fit* ("from nothing, comes nothing") and "what was, will never return," is now broken through. Christian hope is learned hope in that it knows concretely the overwhelming power of the negative and of the judgment over all being and its possibilities, and yet is still hope. As "crucified hope" it can be resurrection hope.

III. DEATH AS CRISIS AND CRITERION

The hope which allies itself with the open possibilities and the favorable tendencies of the world process may be disappointed, but it cannot be destroyed.[9] Indeed, it can and must be disappointed of its very character; otherwise, says Bloch, it would not be hope. First of all, it is open to the front, remains in suspension, is placed in what is changeable, and is therefore connected with the contingent, without which there would be nothing new. Secondly, together with the contingent, the possibility of frustration is also implied in hope. However, since it is "allied with a world which does not renounce itself,"[10] in whose not-yet-determined process neither good nor evil is a foregone conclusion, it accords neither with despair nor with a quietistic certainty. It can be disappointed; yet it can also overcome its historical frustrations by virtue of its own character of suspension and by virtue of the continuous lack of determination in the world process itself. It can be disappointed but not in the end.

The hope of which the Bible speaks, on the other hand, is "hope for what we do not see" (Rom. 8:24-25), "the conviction of things unseen" (Heb. 11:1). Like Bloch's hope, it is not certainty, for it is directed not to the visible, but to what is invisible. Nevertheless, it is not hope in an open possibility, and therefore it does not remain in the suspension of indecisiveness. Since it is hope in the power of God which calls nonbeing into being, it recognizes the beginning in the end. Its way is not the possibility of disappointment, but actual disappointment, for it is a hope which shines out of the denial of all possible hope through the crucifixion of Christ into the Easter appearances. The disciples who experienced the appearances of the risen one were not open and hopeful but were disappointed, refuted, and in flight. In the midst of despair they were

born again into living hope. This hope against hope is kindled by
the God of the exodus and the God of the resurrection of the crucified one. It must develop into an engaged expectation of the future
by grasping in obedience and anticipatory joy the open possibilities
in the world process. But it cannot rest assured that this world
will "renounce itself." Precisely in doing whatever prepares
the way of the future in expectation of the coming of Christ, it
must also be prepared to suffer through the dark night in which
no one can be effective.

The peculiar *aporia* for every thought about hope appears with
death,[11] for with death the "enormous power of the negative"
extends into the midst of life. Marxism becomes silent when it
comes to the possibility of the dialectical averting of the power
of death. Revisions of the Marxist critique of religion are evidently
being made at the present. In this context, esoteric Marxism postu-
lates, with all possible discretion, a hope in the indestructibility
of the core of human existence. Because the core of human existence is "still unrealized" and "not yet processed out," it cannot
be annihilated by death: *Non omnis confundar*. The core of existence has not yet manifested itself in the process. Thus, when faced
with death, it is surrounded by a "protective circle of the not-yet-
alive." "Whenever our existence approaches its core, duration
begins, a permanency which is not torpid but which contains . . .
the new without transience."[12] From a social perspective this is
apparent in "what is indestructible in the consciousness of revolutionary solidarity."[13] That which is immortal in a person lies in
that which is immortal in his or her best intentions. It is the "soul
of future humanity" anticipated in the revolutionary consciousness. Natural death is finally understood as a dying into the open
process of the world. Such a "nature" can "enshrine" within itself
the hoped-for and discovered essence of man.[14] Natural death itself
can become the final fruition of human history and need never
destroy it. This materialistic dialogue with death clearly owes
much to the doctrines of the immortality of the soul, metempsy-
chosis, and the world soul that receives into its own future the
individual souls of men.

In view of the deadliness of death in the context of the Easter
appearances of the crucified one, Christian hope is formulated as

hope in the resurrection of the dead and "life out of death." Therefore Christian hope cannot relativize life and death to an immanent point of indifference in the core of existence or in the core of nature. It finds this point in the transcendent faithfulness of God who is able to create life out of death. Its only guarantee of his divine faithfulness is the history of Christ who died and was raised to become the Lord of the living and the dead. Such a hope takes the total deadliness of death and the finality of the finite seriously and gains the power to endure them.

The strength of esoteric Marxism does not lie in these questions of the primal and the ultimate but in their mediation and translation into the penultimate questions of practice posed by human history. Although it reduces the transcendent hopes of Christianity in order to bring them into life and into an active transformation of the world, it is nevertheless able to stimulate the world-transforming aspect which is implicit in the world-overcoming hope of Christianity. Christian hope must continue to resist the religious reductions which are part of esoteric Marxism, but it should learn from the effects of its history. Ernst Bloch has concentrated this historical examination of the West's reflection on the future on two themes: social utopia and natural law.

"Social utopia was concerned with human happiness and natural law with human dignity. Social utopia painted in advance conditions in which *those who labor and are heavily laden* will find rest; natural law construed conditions in which *those who are humiliated and offended* will find satisfaction."[15] This is a clear reference to the wretched of the earth to whom Jesus promised the kingdom and righteousness of God. It finds its contemporary relevance in a critique of the pure economies with which the welfare states of both East and West try to solve all human problems. Human dignity is not possible without economic liberation any more than economic relief is possible without human rights. Each is mutually dependent on the other. There can be no human dignity without an end to need and no genuinely human happiness without the rights of freedom shown in the "upright carriage" and "raised head." A future of man freed from his alienations therefore can come historically through the overcoming of economic and political need. In dialogue with Christian theology this interpretation of natural law becomes an invitation to examine the problem no longer in a stoical frame of mind but in the light of biblical prophecy. In other words, Christians are asked to see human dignity and existence from the viewpoint of the future announced by God, and, in this way, to join the revolutionary way of conceiving natural law with the eschatological knowledge of divine justice as presented in Pauline theology.

The gospel of the kingdom and of the justice of God in Christ can enter into a cooperative endeavor with social-revolutionary work for "those who labor and are heavily laden" and political work for "those who are humiliated and offended," precisely because it goes beyond this in promising justification of the sinner and the resurrection of the dead. In so doing it can destroy the seeds of resignation which spring up in the course of social-political work and it can itself become a stimulus to creative imagination.

IV.   THE "ATHEISM OF HOPE" AS A CLARIFICATION AND A CHALLENGE

Esoteric Marxism combines *atheism* with its reflection on the future in the world process of modern times. "Atheism," however, is always a relative concept. In this case, it opposes concepts which describe God as the guarantor of prevailing forces in nature and in society. Human activity and creative fantasy are to be seen in all temporally conditioned images of God. Feuerbach pointed out that man was not only accountable to his images of God but that he was himself responsible for them. Ernst Bloch, however, is able to make a distinction between the divine hypostases of human beings and the "empty space" into which they were projected.[16] If the images of God return to man and to the earth from which, by analogy, they were derived, the empty space nevertheless does not collapse. Instead, by virture of its own vehemence, this empty space achieves validity as the "open *topos* of the before-us (*vor-uns*), the *novum,* in which human purposive series find mediation and continuation."[17] In this atheistic dethroning of the worldly-supraworldly and natural-supernatural "God," something else appears: "the future" in all images of that future which was hoped for and sought by men. It is an atheism for the sake of a God whose countenance Christians have long obscured with syn-

cretic images of deities from the pagan world and from philosophers (Pascal). So unrecognizable has this countenance become
that it can be recognized and described only with difficulty. Should
not this atheism persuade Christians and Jews to revise their
syncretic images of God in light of the histories to which they owe
their existence and should they not practice the prohibition of
images also in their thought?

The God of Abraham and the Father of Jesus Christ are known
from a history in which promises open up a new future.[18] The
God of the exodus and the resurrection is the "God of hope"
(Rom. 15:13). He is comprehended where people apprehend the
new reality of his future in the promised freedom from slavery,
exile, and bondage to death. Man has faith in him when, in the
midst of the suffering of history, he recalls God's yet unfulfilled
promises and awaits his faithfulness. Man is obedient to him when
he leaves the "safe fortress" of his social systems and, on the horizon of God's future, devotes himself to the transformation of the
world, thereby entering into history. Such a history is conceived,
experienced, and endured from the perspective of the future, and
its future becomes present in the promises of God. One can even
say that the peculiar mystery and driving power in the concrete
promises of God is the universal rule of God: "The whole earth
is full of his glory" (Isa. 6:3), "that God may be all in all" (1 Cor.
15:28). The divinity of God is revealed only with the coming of
his kingdom, which will be the kingdom of freedom and justice,
of the creature who is no longer estranged, but redeemed and
transfigured. This future of God among men and the whole creation becomes present in the mode in which the future gains power
over the present in promise and experienced hope and decides
what will become of the given actuality. God appears as the power
of the future to contradict the negative elements of existence which
we now experience and to set free the forces to overcome them.
Only in the real transformation of one's own life and of the conditions of life, only by going beyond the given actuality and its bonds
and by changing them does that freedom penetrate history which
opens up its future. In that love which in labor and patience takes
upon itself the pain of the negative, reconciliation and resurrection
enter into history.

Although it is clear that faith in God and expectation of the future are indissoluble in the Old and New Testaments, Christian theology has paid far too little attention to the future as the mode of God's being. The exegetical discoveries of the eschatological nature of the primitive Christian message have not received enough weight because of the pressures of the theological tradition and the social position of Christianity. This form of atheism which looks for a future without God has impinged on a dimension neglected by Christian theology. Now theology is obliged to "make a defense to anyone who calls you to account for the hope that is in you . . ." (1 Pet. 3:15). What better way for theology to do this than to declare that its neglected doctrine at the *end* is actually its *beginning*, that is, to make "eschatology" the very medium of its thought! This means not so much a new version of the *articulus de novissimis*, but rather a "warm stream" of hope in all articles of the Christian faith. If one succeeds in thinking of God and the future together (as is possible when one thinks according to the biblical stories), then one can discover the future in the past, the intended eschaton in the beginning, transformation in reconciliation, the kingdom of God in the resurrection of Christ, and the promise in the gospel. An eschatological ontology will then be able to bring together transient matter with its future, and an eschatological anthropology will be able to bring together mortal human existence with its glorification. This will be possible because in both (and here we have the most important consideration) the power of God's future can be made manifest in nothingness itself.

A Christianity which has for so long believed in God without his future in the world, now will seek, in recognizing the practical responsibility of hope for the future of man and the earth, to shape the possibilities and forces of the contemporary world which arise in an almost unmanageable intensity. It will do this for the sake of a world which is developing toward the future of God. To fit itself for this task Christianity must critically abandon the dictatorship of the social milieus in which it lives. It must be heterodox over against them for the sake of an orthodoxy of a greater future. Only as the salt of the earth, a salt which burns the wounds of the earth (Bernanos), can Christianity prepare the earthly present for the coming salvation of the world which has been opened up in the cross of Christ. Then Christianity will no longer bear the train behind society; instead, it will bear the torch ahead.[19]

NOTES TO CHAPTER THREE

1. For the Christian dialogue with Ernst Bloch, cf. M. Reding, "Utopie, Phantasie, Prophetie. Das Prinzip Hoffnung im Marxismus," in *Frankfurter Hefte* (1961), pp. 8–13; Wolf-Dieter Marsch, *Hoffen Worauf? Auseinandersetzung mit E. Bloch* (Hamburg: Furche-Verlag, 1963); J. Moltmann, "Das Prinzip Hoffnung und die christliche Zuversicht," in *Evangelische Theologie* (1963): 537–557; "Hope and Confidence: A Conversation with Ernst Bloch," in *Religion, Revolution and the Future*, trans. M. Douglas Meeks (New York: Charles Scribner's Sons, 1969), pp. 148–176; and also the contributions of J. Metz, W. Pannenberg, P. Tillich, T. Heim, and J. Moltmann in *Ernst Bloch zu ehren. Beiträge zu seinem Werk*, ed. Siegried Unseld (Frankfurt: Suhrkamp, 1965).
2. *Das Prinzip Hoffnung* I (Frankfurt: Suhrkamp, 1959), pp. 235 ff.
3. Ibid., p. 254.
4. Ibid., p. 225.
5. Ibid., p. 234.
6. The question of a negative dialectic has been posed in relation to *Das Prinzip Hoffnung*, and in many quarters. Cf. Wolf-Dieter Marsch, *Hoffen Worauf?* p. 99: "Has he not reduced the gravity of the negative, for example, by interpreting the destructive power of nothingness as a 'not-yet' of that which is possible, but as yet unrealized?" Similarly, A. Löwe, *Ernst Bloch zu ehren*, note 1, p. 141: "I must ask you, as I ask myself, whether all your explanations do justice to the entire force of dead nothingness, to the lasting threat of ultimate meaninglessness, after which there is no resurrection?" A similar question was raised by T. Adorno, "Blochs Spuren," in *Noten zur Literatur* II (Frankfurt: Suhrkamp, 1961), pp. 131 ff. The references are to Bloch's "Einsichten in den Nihilismus," in *Philosophische Grundfragen I: Zur Ontologie des Noch-Nicht-Seins* (Frankfurt: Suhrkamp, 1961), pp. 41 ff.
7. Ibid., p. 63.
8. Ibid., p. 74.
9. "Kann Hoffnung enttäuscht werden?" in *Verfremdungen* I (Frankfurt: Suhrkamp, 1962), pp. 211 ff.
10. *Tübinger Einleitung in die Philosophie* II (Frankfurt: Suhrkamp, 1964), p. 177.
11. *Das Prinzip Hoffnung* II, par. 52, "Hoffnungsbilder gegen den Tod," pp. 1297 ff.
12. Ibid., p. 1391.
13. Ibid., p. 1381.
14. Ibid., pp. 1383 ff.
15. *Naturrecht und menschliche Würde* (Frankfurt: Suhrkamp, 1961), p. 13.
16. *Das Prinzip Hoffnung* II, pp. 1524–1525.
17. Ibid., p. 1530.

18. Cf., on what follows, my *Theology of Hope* (1967); also the contributions of Wolfhart Pannenberg and Johannes Metz in *Ernst Bloch zu ehren* (Frankfurt: Suhrkamp, 1965).
19. This image was originally created by Kant to illustrate the Enlightenment refusal of the part played by philosophy as the handmaid of theology. Bloch took it up later (*Tübinger Einleitung* II, p. 30). It is very apt: (1) in order to illustrate the role of Christianity, which serves the world by serving the coming kingdom of God, and (2) in order to determine the role of a theology of the divine promise.

IV.

Introduction to the "Theology of Hope"

I. THE CONTEXT AND THE TEXT

Every theology undoubtedly has its historical context. Technological development produced in the sixties a new sensibility for an open future. Futurology and the sciences of planning and projection arose everywhere. The Kennedy era awakened in America and elsewhere a secular enthusiasm for hope which was politically active in the civil rights movement and in the Peace Corps. Also in the lands bogged down by Stalinist bureacracy in the well-established ruts of Marxism, a new hope for a "socialism with a human face" arose, as in the case of Alexander Dubček in Czechoslovakia. In Catholicism, the Second Vatican Council aroused a great hope for a new church open to the world, and in 1968, at Uppsala, the ecumenical movement took as its motto the words of promise, "Behold, I make all things new." We are indebted to the sixties for drawing us out of apathy and giving us the will for a new freedom in many areas of life. It cannot be denied that in this context also belongs the rapid dissemination of a "theology of hope" into many lands.

But the context is not yet the *text* itself. If one knows the historical context of a theology, it does not necessarily follow that one knows its specific text. In order to become acquainted with it, one must enter into the real concern of theology itself. The first factor is the *time* in which one lives. The other is the *concern* for which one lives. The one is the *circumstances* in which one thinks; the other is the *substance* of one's thoughts.

In these reflections I do not want to rekindle the ashes of a time which is past, but to strive to keep a flame burning. For that reason

I am not speaking about the context, but about the text of the theology of hope, namely, the Bible.

For a Christian theology of hope, this hope is not a modern phenomenon which must be interpreted religiously, but the subject and the motivation for theology itself. It is not grounded in optimism, but in faith. It is not a theology *about* hope, but a theology growing *out of* hope in God. The basis for this hope does not lie in the ups and downs of the moods of the time, but in the promise of the coming God. These promises of God have been incarnated in the promissory history of Israel and in the promissory history of Jesus of Nazareth. The writings in the Old and New Testaments comprise the history book of God's promises. The Bible tells the story of God's hope which will be fulfilled in the whole world. It does not relate its story in the manner of a teller of fairytales—"once upon a time . . ."—or of a modern historian who wants to know how it "really was then" (Ranke). It recounts the past in such a way that through it a new future and freedom for the hearers are inaugurated. It reveals the future in the past and makes God's hope present by means of the remembrance of his historical association with Israel, the covenant, and with Jesus Christ, the incarnation. It recounts the story of the anticipations of God's future in the past and makes what is open, incomplete, and unsatisfied in this past a matter of real concern again.

A theology which has hope as its internal motor is therefore an interpretation of the biblical promissory history for the understanding of the present-day mission of Christianity in the world. Hope is not the opposite of remembrance, for there are dangerous and liberating memories which crowd in upon our present and place it in question by warning us of an unattained future. They hinder our being satiated and satisfied or despairing and resigned in coming to terms with the power of given facts. In this regard, the Bible has dangerous as well as liberating memories of hope in store for us.

Some day the biblical theology of "it is written" will become an ontology of "it has taken place." Some day, in nature, in history, and in society, we will no longer encounter temptations and contradictions but confirmation of what has been promised. Some day, promise and reality, hope and experience will be in accord.

But as long as that has not happened, as long as "all the tears" are not wiped away, as long as suffering follows suffering and guilt is piled upon guilt, for just this long the twain will not come into agreement. For just this long we should abide by "what is written," namely, the promise, and we should value hope more than experiential reality.

If we begin to read the Bible as the book of God's hope, then we will find that it is a highly revolutionary and subversive book. The hope about which it speaks is valid for the hopeless and not for the optimists. It is valid for the poor and not for the rich. It is valid for the downtrodden and the insulted so that they will raise up their heads. It is valid for the oppressed so that they will learn to walk uprightly, and all this as it will be in heaven, so already here on this earth. As the book of the promises of God, the Bible is not a document of an ancient religion but still has its time ahead of it. It points beyond itself into the future which does not yet fill our present. Christian theology exists for the purpose not of following after the *Zeitgeist* and bearing its train, but for carrying before it the torch of hope and enkindling the fire of criticism in lazy humanity.

II. THE GOD OF HOPE

Christian theology speaks of God *historically*. It speaks of "the God of Abraham, Isaac, and Jacob," and it speaks of "the Father of Jesus Christ." It connects talk about God with remembrance of *historical persons*. Christian theology speaks of "the God of the exodus" as in the First Commandment and of "the God who raised Jesus from the dead," as in the Easter gospel. It combines belief in God with remembrance of these *historical events* and *root experiences*.

But Christian theology speaks of this history *eschatologically*. That is, it proclaims the "God of Abraham" as the God of the promise of blessing for *all* people. It expects from the God of the exodus a future in which *all* lands will be full of his majesty and beauty. It proclaims the "Father of Jesus Christ" as the *one* God of *all* men and his coming kingdom as the liberation of the whole groaning creation from its misery. This is what is special and unique in the biblical message about God. It is not a metaphysics

of the highest being, but it emerges from history and has the
future and the end of history, that is liberation, as its goal. It is a
belief in God, which is harnessed between memory and hope.
Therefore, this language about God cannot be abstract and without a history, but it must be a concrete and liberating language.
By awakening hope in the coming of God through remembrance
of history, it inaugurates a new history and new freedom for men.

What is meant then by "history"? Paul in Rom. 4:11 and the
author of the Epistle to the Hebrews in chapter 11:8–19 call
Abraham the "father of faith." From the course of Abraham's life
it becomes clear what happens to men who follow the God of hope.
This example makes clear for the first time that "history" means
exodus.

In Josh. 24:2–3, we read the following:

"Your fathers lived of old beyond the Euphrates . . . and they served
other gods. Then I took your father Abraham from beyond the River
and led him through all the land of Canaan. . . ."

Gen. 12:1–2 tells this story. The "Lord" whom Abraham did not
know commanded him:

"Go from your country and your kindred and your father's house to
the land that I will show you. And I will make of you a great nation,
and I will bless you, and make your name great, so that you will be a
blessing."

So Abraham experienced this reality of God in which he
heard his promise and followed it. How and why, it is not said.
Evidently he trusted in the word of promise more than in all the
securities of his life "beyond the River." He left the familiar pat-
terns of his life which had provided a home and security for him.
He abandoned his fatherland and became an alien. He left his
friends and was alone. He left his father's house and lost his identity. He left even his gods, these Aramaic nature gods who guaranteed order, fertility, and peace in the "eternal return of the same,"
and became a godless person who alone followed the call of the
unknown "Lord." The Bible calls this "faith": leaving the dwelling places of reality where one has peace and security and giving
oneself over to the course of history, to the way of freedom and

danger, the way of disappointment and surprise, borne along and led solely by God's hope.

Analogously, the tribes of Israel experienced in Egypt the reality of Yahweh in promise and exodus. As Exodus 3 reports, on Mount Sinai Moses was given the promise and mission of leading his people out of slavery and the fleshpots of Egypt into a far land "flowing with milk and honey." He asked for the name of this God and received the answer, which has remained a riddle ever since: "I am who I am" (Ex. 3:14). This means that this God does not make himself known by his name or bind himself to a place, or subject himself to religious magic in order to prevent men from swearing by him as they did by other gods. The expression "I am who I am," emphasizes the subjectivity and sovereignty of God who can never become the object and idol of men. Martin Buber and Karl Barth have correctly understood this.

But this formula for God can also be translated: "I will be who I will be." It also contains the future of God. Ernst Bloch is right, therefore, when he speaks of a "God who has the future as the mode of his being" (*Das Prinzip Hoffnung*, II, p. 1458). This is a *novum* with respect to the Aramaic, Egyptian, and Greek divinities, which are all "eternal" and timeless. With this God of the exodus, however, the future must be especially considered as the mode of this existing. "I will be who I will be" sets out the direction in which his presence must be sought. One can also translate it as "I will be with you." Whoever follows his promise and mission will experience God's nearness and faithfulness as one who travels with him going ahead of him. Israel thus left Egypt trusting in the one "who will be there," wherever they went. With this expectation they experienced the miracle of the Sea of Reeds as a demonstration of his faithfulness to his promise. He who had promised that he would "be there" was there, and thereafter in Israel whoever was supposed to tell his children who was the God of the fathers and the God of the exodus had to tell this story of promise, faithfulness, and fulfillment. In Israel there were no images and no abstract concepts of God. Here God was understood through remembered history and remembered history led to hope for the coming history. The First Commandment summarized this: "I am the Lord your God, who brought you out of the land of

Egypt, out of the house of bondage. You shall have no other gods before me " (Ex. 20:2–3).

What then do we mean by a promise? A promise is a pledge that proclaims a reality which is not yet at hand. A promise pledges a new future, and in the promise this new future is already *word-present*. If a divine promise is involved, it means that this future does not result from those possibilities which are already inherent in the present, but that it originates from God's creative possibilities. God's promise always points to a new creation as the word for divine "creation" in the Old Testament, *barah,* indicates. *Barah* is used more often for the creation of a new future in history than for the creation of all things in the beginning, for history is a creative process. The *word* of the promise itself already creates something new. It is not a word which is indicative of existing realities and possibilities. By promising a new future, it simultaneously commends men to seek this future. Only he who seeks finds. This distinguishes biblical promise from Cassandra's prophecies about the future and from modern prognoses about the year 2000. Promises point to fulfillment and hope expects the fulfillment of the faithfulness of God who cannot belie himself.

If one puts one's trust in God, the scheme of promise and fulfillment should not become legalistically dogmatic, for the expectation of fulfillment remains open for moments of *surprise.* A multitude of God's promises was transmitted to Israel in its history. Many are said to have been fulfilled, others were simply left behind by history, and still others were interpreted anew and expanded through partial fulfillment. Thus Israel sought the "land flowing with milk and honey" but found only Palestine where not only milk and honey were flowing but certainly also blood and tears. This was not the fulfillment of all hopes, but it was still something. Israel interpreted such experiences of partial fulfillment as an earnest of even greater hopes, as the pledge of an even greater future. Concerning this, Gerhard von Rad says:

Here everything is in motion, the accounts never balance, and fulfillment unexpectedly gives rise in turn to another promise of something greater still. Here nothing has its ultimate meaning in itself, but is always an earnest of something still greater. (*Old Testament Theology,* II, pp. 116–117)

What is the source of placing this *surplus value of hope* above all historical experiences, even above the experience of historical fulfillment? It appears to me that in all the individual hopes there was an anticipation, not just of the land, of security, and of an inheritance, but of God's future itself. Therefore, the finite promises point beyond themselves to the eschatological final arrival of *God himself*. For ultimately, the *author* and the *content* of the promise are one, and the different fulfillments in history which attest to the promises are all manifested forms of this one final future in which God himself dwells with all people. Therefore, one often finds in the Psalms the simple statement, "We hope in God."

How can we understand this "God of hope," a God with the future as the mode of his being?

Christian theology very early endeavored to describe the divinity of God in terms of Greek metaphysics. Therefore historical discourse about the "coming God" was displaced by abstract discourse about the "eternal God," who is enthroned in heaven in complete holiness, while men suffer on earth, die, and disappear forever. The place of the historical "faithfulness of God" to his promises was therefore taken by the metaphysical determination of the essential immutability of God (*immutabilitas Dei*), in contrast to all variable things on earth. Contemporary atheism is not alone in its protest against this theism of divine omnipotence and heavenly authority, and primarily for two reasons: (1) Where such a super-authority is in control, there is no room for freedom, not even the freedom of the children of God. Either there is such a God, in which case, man is not free; or man is free, in which case there can be no such God. (2) If God is omnipotent, why then do guiltless children suffer and die? If God is omnipotent, the misery of the earth proves he is not good; or he is good, but then obviously not omnipotent. The question of freedom and the outcry of suffering are the bases for every serious atheism which resists banality.

If we follow the biblical discourse about the "God of hope," we will have to give prominence to the *future as the mode of God's existence with us*. God is not present in the same way that the things in the world are at hand. God, like his kingdom, is coming and only as the coming one, as future, is he already present. He is already present in the way in which his future in promise and hope empowers the present. He is, however, not yet present in the manner of his eternal presence. Understood as the *coming one* and as the *power of the future*, God is experienced as the *ground of liberation*, and not as the enemy of freedom. He lifts man above the present palpable reality and liberates him from the systems of the existing world and contemporary society. As the power of the exodus, his promise causes men in hope to grow beyond themselves. For freedom consists in going beyond what is as such, even beyond what one is in himself, in order creatively to seize the new possibilities of the future. The "God of hope" was from the beginning a liberating God. The transcendence of his future can be understood as the basis for the human transcending of every historical present. We should, therefore, not exchange Yahweh for Baal, but rather destroy the idols of domination, authority, superiority, law and order, to be able to find again the God of the exodus as the power of the future, as the strength of freedom and the source of the *novum*.

Now many have said that it is one-sided to emphasize only the future as God's mode of existing. God is just as much also in the past and in the present as he is in the future, they say. There is a misunderstanding here with respect to the "future" which is intended. The Greeks usually described the eternity of their gods in such a way that they spoke of the presence of the gods in the past, present, and future: "Zeus was, Zeus is, and Zeus will be"; ergo, Zeus is eternal. When the Marxists celebrated the Lenin centennial, they produced the following apotheosis: "Lenin lived, Lenin lives, Lenin will live." Men have always deified their idols in this manner. If we understand time and eternity like this, then, of course, the future cannot be valued very highly.

In the New Testament, however, there is no such understanding of time and eternity. In the book of Revelation 1:4, we read: "Grace to you and peace from him who is and who was and who is to come."

One expects that in the third part it would read ". . . and *who will be*." This would correspond to the eternal and continually present God. But instead of the future of the verb *einai* (to be), here we find the future of *erchesthai* (to come). This is decisive.

God's future is not that he will be as he is and was, but that he comes. The future is, therefore, not a dimension of his eternity, but is his own movement in which he comes to us. This gives the future of God a preeminence over his past and his present in history. His actions in history in the past and the present are aimed at his coming and attain their significance from his future. Who God in himself is will be revealed then. We know about God here only in an historically provisional way.

If we understand God in this way as the power of a new future, then we must accordingly change our understanding of the future. We have two possible ways of speaking of it. We speak of that which *will be* and of that which *is coming*. A profound distinction is involved here. We can calculate what will be in its possibility and probability from the factors and tendencies of the present. For example, we observe the process of development and estimate the growth rate of industry and the population increase for the next twenty years. In this way futurology and planning protract the present into the future. Here the future is that which is already pregnant in the present. This way of thinking about the future works with the method of extrapolation.

It is a different matter, however, when we ask about that which is coming. We do not look then from the present into the future, but from the future into the present. We do not *extrapolate* the future out of the present; rather we *anticipate* the future in the present. We do not have the feeling that we must plan the future but rather that we must be responsible for the present in face of the future. We hope for coming well-being and we are anxious in the face of coming death. Children eagerly anticipate Christmas and we call the time of joyful anticipation and preparation for Christmas Advent. That which is coming throws forward its shadows and it already has its effect on the present through excited hope and awakened fear.

Just how profound the distinction is between these two ways of treating the future becomes clear in reference to etymological considerations. In French there are two words for future: *futur* and *avenir*. The German word *Zukunft* translates not the Latin word *futurum* but the Latin word *adventus*, whose Greek equivalent is *parousia*. *Adventus* designates *that which is coming*. If we apply this to theology we are not able to speak of a "becoming God" but only of the "coming God." This is the difference between eschatology and process philosophy. If we speak of the "coming God," his future becomes the source of the times. His coming constantly creates new time in history. If his creation at the end of history means "Behold, I make all things new," we are able to anticipate in it that his grace is "new every morning."

In practice, of course, we always combine what we hope shall come with what is and what can become. We combine what we hope for and want with what we are subjectively able to do and what is objectively possible. But theoretically we must distinguish the two. The sciences give us what we wish, but they do not tell us what we should wish. Thus Albert Einstein was right when he said: "Science without religion is blind; it doesn't know where to go. And religion without science is lame; it doesn't know how to go." It seems to me that with this realization the fruitfulness of the eschatological, anticipating thinking of hope has become clear not only for theology, but also for scientific and political practice.

III.   THE MESSIAH OF HOPE

Let us now turn back to the text of the theology of hope and ask whether the future orientation of this theology is also in accordance with the New Testament.

When Jesus of Nazareth first appeared in public he proclaimed God by preaching that "the kingdom of God has come near." He drew radical consequences from this. His proclamation was therefore an *eschatological proclamation.* The Gospels summarize his message in three points: "The kingdom of God has come near. Repent. And believe in the gospel."

The word "kingdom" means a future in which God is finally and completely present, in which men receive their freedom in God, and in which all the misery of the creation is overcome. The "gospel" here is the word which is the communicating medium between this future and the present. "Repentance" here means the radical transformation of persons and circumstances so that they are turned around to face God's future. "Faith" here is the acceptance of the freedom for the coming kingdom offered in the Word.

The proclamation of Jesus is in the form of *eschatological anticipation*. It has a thoroughly proleptic thrust, for Jesus anticipates through his words, his deeds, and his life shared with other persons, what, according to the Old Testament expectancy, can only happen on the last day. He does already today what is supposed to come tomorrow. He lives entirely from the nearness of God's future. He can be properly understood, therefore, as the anticipator of the coming of God and the liberator of a bound humanity.

Because of the content of its message, the proclamation of Jesus breaks through the late Jewish expectation of justice and the kingdom of God. Jesus did not promise the kingdom to the just and judgment to the unjust, as was usually the case, but clearly and preferentially promises the kingdom to the poor and the unjust, not because of their injustice, but because of God's grace. Jesus proclaimed the kingdom of God as prevenient and unconditional grace to the sinners and tax collectors, and his blessedness to the poor, to those who were grieving, and to those who were hungry. He announced the kingdom, not as judgment but as joy. He celebrated its arrival in the "banquet for the just" with unjust sinners. He distributed the kingdom in the forgiveness of sins. This is what is so astonishingly new in the message of Jesus. Accordingly, he distanced himself from John the Baptist, from whom he had probably come to know the message of the near kingdom. The eschatology of Jesus is not the preaching of judgment, but the realization of pure grace and freedom. Therefore, his disciples did not fast and, to the continual indignation of many Christians also, he was known as a "glutton and wine-bibber." ·

What right did Jesus have and what power did he use to introduce this astonishing and disarming message of the open and gracious future of God?

Obviously, he renounced all the religious institutions of his people and did not call on the traditions of their holy history. He relied completely and exclusively on the future of God, whom he called "my Father." With the claim "But I say to you . . ." in the antitheses of the Sermon on the Mount, he placed himself above the authority of Moses as no prophet had done previously. By forgiving sins, he did what was reserved for God alone. We do not historically know who Jesus considered himself to be. But his total appearance shows that someone greater than Moses and the prophets was intended here, greater also than the figures of apocalyptic expectation, such as "the Messiah" and the "Son of man." Otherwise, Jesus could not have identified the coming kingdom of God with his own person: "And Blessed is he who takes no offense at me." This means that his claim to power received no support from the past, but was totally directed toward confirmation by God in the future. His right to make such a claim hung, so to speak, "in the air." He based this claim on nothing, or rather on God himself.

For that same reason, Jesus' own poverty and powerlessness were manifestly vulnerable. The annoying thing about Jesus lay not in his anticipation of the kingdom of God but in the humbleness of his person: the son of a carpenter from Nazareth without temporal glory or might, he anticipated God's glorious kingdom among those who were powerless and wretched. This is what constituted the scandal which led to his condemnation. The inner contradiction between Jesus' claim of anticipating God's kingdom and his own poverty, as well as his associations with the outcasts and poor, characterizes his historical appearance in general. His love brought God to the godless, but his love could not hinder the pious from taking offense at him. Jesus' eschatology of the coming God is, therefore, a highly dialectical eschatology. It is the preaching of the *kingdom* without any might or majesty by the *poor* Jesus of Nazareth which led to his crucifixion. I believe that only in the light of his resurrection from this death on the cross is the riddle of his life solved. That is, only through the poverty, the humbleness, and the love of Jesus can God's kingdom of majesty and freedom come to those who are poor, abandoned, and enslaved.

With this we come to the second, that is to say, the other side of the story of Jesus. The historical Jesus anticipated the kingdom of God among the poor, the righteousness of God among those without rights, and the glory of God among the sick and the lepers. He was condemned as a blasphemer and crucified because he practiced the justice of grace and, thereby, violated the religious as well as the political law and order. No one would recall this man from Nazareth today, if it had not dawned on the disciples that in the Easter appearances God had made himself known to the crucified Jesus and in his resurrection had already begun his future in him. According to all that we know, Easter is the historical origin and the continuing basis of the Christian faith, the Christian church, and the Christian hope. In the light of Easter, however, the early Christian proclamation was, once more, eschatological and thus proleptic proclamation of the coming of God.

In the late Jewish hope, the general resurrection of the dead was definitely an integral part of the expectation of God. In the latter days, God will raise the dead and reveal in this way his power over death. When it is then proclaimed that God has raised this dead Jesus from the dead, nothing less is asserted than that this future of God has broken into the midst of the history of death in this one person. Thus for all who hear this proclamation, their expectancy of a distant end becomes the certain hope of a near future. The first titles used by Christians to describe the special status of Jesus were all proleptic: "the first fruits of those who have fallen asleep"; "the first fruits . . . of the resurrection"; and the "author of life." Easter was understood as the actual anticipation of God's future and, therefore, became the basis for certainty in the hope for resurrection. But this again is only the one side.

The resurrection of the dead, according to late Jewish hope, was seen in the horizon of the final judgment of God according to the law. Resurrection then does not have to be something good, because, according to Dan. 12:2, all will awaken from the dead, but "some to everlasting life, and some to shame and everlasting contempt." The just will enter into eternal life, but the unjust, into condemnation. For the latter, resurrection is, therefore, not something to be anticipated. It would be better if they would remain dead. Here the law still reigns over the resurrection of the dead. And since no one knows whether he is really just or unjust, resurrection is a very ambiguous hope for every person.

But this is not the case in the Christian hope. Who was it that was resurrected according to the Christian Easter message? One who was correctly condemned according to the divine law of Israel as a blasphemer. One who not without reason was crucified according to the order of the *Pax Romana* as a political agitator. The new and astonishing factor in the Christian message is not that someone was granted precedence in the resurrection of the dead over all others or not even deliverance from death as such. Judaism also spoke of special deliverance from death of particularly right-eous men like Elijah and Enoch. The resurrection of the cursed, outcast, and crucified Jesus is the unbelievable factor in the Chris-tian faith. The question is not whether or not resurrection is pos-sible but rather whether the just God could have raised this blasphemer and agitator from the dead. Paul saw the consequences most clearly. If Jesus died on the cross cursed by the law, then his resurrection means redemption from the curse of the law (Gal. 3:13). And Christ becomes the "end of the law, that every one who has faith may be justified" (Rom. 10:4). Therefore if God raised this crucified one from the dead, he has revealed a new justice, namely, the justice of unconditional grace, which creates rights for those who have none, accepts the godless, and seeks out the lost.

The resurrection of the dead within the framework of the law's righteousness is a two-edged sword, as we have seen. The resurrec-tion of the crucified Christ, however, reveals a new justice, which is the justification of the godless. The hope in resurrection within Christianity is therefore no longer ambiguous, but straightforward and clear. It faces without fear God's future as a joyous hope in the power of divine grace, which *even death cannot resist*. It is indeed a hope for the hopeless. Through the crucified Christ the future of resurrection and life, of freedom, joy, and justice is opened up to those who live in guilt without hope and who must die in fear without a future. To say it simply, the resurrection of the crucified Christ revealed the kingdom of the coming God as the power of anticipatory love. This love has no conditions placed on it and knows no boundaries. Through the love manifested in the resurrection that which is hateful is rendered lovable. Thus hope is disseminated for the hopeless. The future is inaugurated, not by way of examples and commands, but through the love, the patience, and the sacrifice of God.

I will conclude this section with the following thesis: The cross of Christ is the sign of God's hope on earth for all those who live here in the shadow of the cross. Theology of hope is at its hard core theology of the cross. The cross of Christ is the presently given form of the kingdom of God on earth. In the crucified Christ we view the future of God. Everything else is dreams, fantasies, and mere wish images. Hope born out of the cross of Christ distinguishes Christian faith from superstition as well as from disbelief. The freedom generated by the cross distinguishes Christian faith from optimism as well as from terrorism.

IV. THE CONGREGATION OF HOPE

In this final section I want to speak about the "congregation of hope." But I do not intend to give existing churches and congregations a new religious ideology on which they can base their previous practice. The hope of which I speak is to be seen in "the sons of Abraham," who have executed an exodus from those religious and political establishments which oppress the world today.

Abraham left his fatherland and his gods. He became a free man and an alien for the sake of the promise of a blessing for all peoples. Israel abandoned religious and political captivity in Egypt in order to find the land of freedom and righteousness. True Christianity follows the man of Nazareth who was crucified by the priests and politicians of his people and by the imperial power of Rome. Real Christians are not "conformed to this world," as Paul says in Rom. 12:2, but are "transformed by the renewal of their minds." "For," as Heb. 13:14 reminds us, "here we have no lasting city," neither in Rome nor in Germany nor in America, "but we seek the city which is to come." But where does this "promised land" lie? Where should we go?

In earlier times, millions of people went to America, to the "new world." They emigrated out of the oppressive circumstances in Europe in order to find a "land of unlimited possibilities" or "a new order of things" and sometimes also "the new Jerusalem," Philadelphia. This was an impossible dream. The country "Utopia," where "peace and justice kiss each other," simply does not exist on any of the maps of the earth. "The "new world" is not to be found somewhere on the globe. Where should one emigrate to? It is basically the same everywhere.

For the Jews there was and is, of course, the land of their fathers, the land of God. For Christians, there never was such a land. The hope of Christians was different from the beginning. Certainly they too are under way and have no "lasting city," but their hope is not directed toward another better land—rather toward another new future for all countries. Therefore they do not emigrate from one land to another throughout the expanses of the earth, but throughout the vast eras of history.

One does not move to another country to find freedom and God. One remains where one is in order to correspond to the conditions of the coming kingdom of God through the renewal of the heart and by practical transformation of social circumstances. The front line of the exodus is not emigration, but liberation through the transformation of the present. For in the present, where we always are, the powers of the past wrestle with the powers of the future, and fear and hope struggle for domination. By changing ourselves and the circumstances around us, by anticipating the future God, we emigrate out of the past into the future.

V.

Jewish and Christian Messianism

I. "ARE YOU THE ONE WHO IS COMING?"

In the messianic question of the "coming one" Judaism and Christianity are intimately united. In the answer which each hears they seem to be divided in the deepest way. "The coming one" is the veiled cipher for the promised *Messiah* and the expected *Son of man*.[1] The Messiah seems to be the King of the end time who restores Israel and through Zion brings righteousness and peace to the nations. He is often characterized by Christian scholars too narrowly as the "exponent of national Jewish eschatology."[2] The Son of man, according to Daniel 7, is supposed to be a preexistent heavenly being. After the destruction of the bestial kingdoms of the world, he brings from God the universal kingdom "of man."[3] Scholarship often ascribes historical redemption to the Messiah, while assigning redemption from history to the Son of man. Yet in Jewish apocalyptic both figures of hope were fused with each other in such a way that a two-dimensional messiology emerged: the Messiah represented the immanent and the Son of man the transcendent side of the mediation of God's kingdom.[4]

Both figures of hope, however, are shadowy and lack a definite character because they must be transparent for him whose future they are to mediate. Thus in prophecy the expression "the coming one" was used for God himself, e.g., Isa. 35:4ff.: "Behold, your God will come . . . and save you. Then the eyes of the blind shall be opened, and the ears of the deaf unstopped; then shall the lame man leap like a hart, and the tongue of the dumb sing for joy." The coming God brings the liberation of man and peace for the creation.[5] Conversely, therefore, redemption, liberation, and salvation can be understood as signs for the nearness of God. It is true that Jewish hope looks for the "signs of the time," but it defends itself against messianic personality cults and the fixation of the "coming one" on utopian images, for it expects the coming one in faithfulness to the Torah.

The question of the "coming one" was one of the basic questions asked of Jesus of Nazareth. Matthew depicts Jesus' answer as indirect: "Go and tell John what you hear and see: the blind receive their sight and the lame walk, lepers are cleansed and the deaf hear, and the dead are raised up, and the poor have good news preached to them. And blessed is he who takes no offense at me" (11:4–6). Luke summarizes the mission of Jesus with the signs of the promise's fulfillment in Isa. 61:1–2: ". . . to preach good news to the poor . . . to proclaim release to the captives and recovering of sight to the blind, to set at liberty those who are oppressed, to proclaim the acceptable year of the Lord" (4:18–19). The liberations which happen through the deeds and proclamations of Jesus speak for themselves. They are the signs of the messianic time. To those who experience and believe them, he reveals himself as the "coming one."[6] On the other hand, with his messianic mission he represents the coming God and his kingdom. Jesus' answer to John the Baptist's question is indirect because the observation of the messianic time is a question of faith. But Jesus binds the awakening of this messianic faith to his human person and to the shape of his suffering: "Blessed is he who takes no offense at me." With this, the question. Are you the coming one or shall we look for another? is given back to the liberating experience of those who are suffering with Jesus and to their faith.

II. JEWISH OBJECTIONS

At this point arises the objection of those who "wait for another."

The Jew has a profound knowledge of the unredeemedness of the world and he acknowledges no enclaves of redemption in the midst of this unredeemed world. The conception of a redeemed soul in the midst of an unredeemed world is utterly alien to his being, and inaccessible to him because of the very ground of his existence. This is the real cause for the rejection of Jesus by Israel, not a merely external, national conception of messianism.[7]

This may be right in view of the later doctrines of the church, but do the poor who have good news preached to them, the sick

who are healed, the outcasts who are accepted really understand
themselves as "redeemed souls" in an unredeemed world?

Judaism, in all its forms and manifestations, has always maintained a
conception of redemption as an event which takes place publicly, on
the stage of history and within the community. It is an occurrence
which takes place in the visible world. . . . In contrast, Christianity
conceives of redemption as an event in the spiritual and unseen realm,
an event which is reflected in the soul, in the private world of each
individual, and which effects an inner transformation which need not
correspond to anything outside. . . . The reinterpretation of the prophetic promises of the Bible to refer to a realm of inwardness . . .
always seemed to the religious thinkers of Judaism to be an illegitimate
anticipation of something which at best could be seen as the interior
side of an event basically taking place in the external world, but could
never be cut off from the event itself.[8]

But is the primal faith of the redeemed and forgiven really such
an interiorization of salvation? It is true that in historical Christianity there has often been a substitution of realistic, messianic
hope with spiritualizing and individualizing notions of salvation.[9]
Yet Judaism as well as Christianity has been able to maintain only
with the greatest difficulty the realism and universalism of its hope
against the influence of gnosticism. It thus cannot be the case that
"a totally different concept of redemption determines the attitude
to Messianism in Judaism and in Christianity."[10] It seems to me
that the difference lies in the eschatological experience of time
which does or does not occur in Jesus. The question of the Baptist
is the question about the messianic *kairos*. If it is a question of
time, the form of the messianic anticipation of redemption in this
still unredeemed world is further determined by the claim of the
hope which originates in it. Is it the Torah of Moses or the gospel
of Christ? For whom does the Torah speak and for whom the
gospel?

In the conflict over the messiahship of Jesus, Christianity and
Judaism have developed a wide gulf between themselves to the
detriment of both. "For the Jews the Messiah threatens to disappear behind the kingdom of God. For the Christian church the
kingdom of God threatens to disappear behind the figure of the
Messiah."[11] A hope in the kingdom of God without messianic

presence in history will lead to an expectation of world catastrophe, for "this world cannot bear the righteousness of the kingdom." Conversely, a messianic presence without hope in the kingdom of God as its consummation will become illusory and overlook the "mystery of evil." Christian Christology should no longer cause Judaism to suspect the hope of the Messiah nor should the Jewish expectation of the kingdom cause Christians to suspect a real futuristic eschatology.

III. THE MESSIAH AS SUFFERER

Jewish messiology[12] knows not only restorative and utopian hopes in the "coming one" who either will restore "life with the Fathers" or will establish the New Jerusalem. The apocalyptic traditions speak also of his coming as incalculable and undeserved. He comes unexpectedly and, for many, only when all hope is extinguished in suffering. Furthermore he comes in hiddenness and therefore might be present already but unrecognized. According to the legends, he was born on the day of the Temple's destruction. In preparation of his day he has since then wandered unrecognized among the nations of the earth. His initial appearance is basically that of the sufferer. He lives among beggars and lepers. He suffers with the persecuted of Israel. Correspondingly, the day of messianic liberation is ushered in through the "birth pangs of the Messiah," through apocalyptic distress and the horrors of the destruction. Christian faith does not distinguish itself but rather finds a common ground with Judaism in recognizing the messiahship of Jesus not only in his mission and the signs and wonders accompanying it but even more in his way of suffering, in his vulnerability and powerlessness, and finally in his death as an outcast. Although only a few Jewish texts speak of a suffering and dying Messiah—and indeed none points to a Messiah condemned by the law—there is a sufficient correspondence present in the Job figure of the Jewish people and in its own history of suffering.[13]

The suffering and dying of Jesus was understood as the suffering and dying of the "coming one" and was thus depicted with apocalyptic colors. Because one understood him as an eschatological person, one perceived in his destiny the anticipation of the end and of the judgment at the end time. But if the judgment which is coming upon everyone is already executed on this one, then he has suffered it representatively and for the sake of all others. To understand the death of Jesus in the messianic categories, under which he set out and through which he is comprehended since Easter, means to understand him as an eschatological suffering act of God's love approaching the "dead."[14] Through the suffering of the Messiah, the suffering ones receive messianic hope. Through the sacrifice of the Messiah, "those who have been given up" (Rom. 1:26)—Jews and Gentiles—receive freedom for eternal life. Through his acting *for them* in the judgment, the sinners become just *in him*. Christian faith therefore has understood the powerless suffering and the forsaken dying of Jesus, not as refutation of his messianic hope, but rather as its deepest realization under the conditions of a godless and inhuman world which stands under the coming judgment. It has therefore discovered the hope of the suffering ones in the suffering of this "coming one." It has found the liberation of the guilty ones in the death of this guiltless one.

IV.   HISTORY AS CRISIS

In Christianity as in Judaism there is a constant ambivalence between apocalyptic expectation of catastrophes and utopian enthusiasm of fulfillment. The pathos of modernity still reveals an ambivalence between secularized faith in progress and secularized fear of catastrophes. In the messianic understanding of Jesus, however, this ambivalence has been overcome. Insofar as his dying is the representative anticipation of judgment, his resurrection is the real beginning and the first glimpse of righteousness, of life, and of the kingdom. The element of danger is involved in the anticipation and the first glimpse itself. "Where danger comes near, the rescue also emerges" (Hölderlin) can mean in a Jewish sense: "When the whole of Israel no longer keeps the Sabbath," or "when you have sunk to the lowest level," the Messiah will come.[15] But in view of the anticipation of the end and its change from judgment to grace in the destiny of Jesus, we must also say: "Where the rescue comes near, the danger emerges."[16] The messianic "history in postponement" becomes in view of Jesus the messianic crisis. A Christianity which understands Jesus in this way should be conscious of itself as being "a ferment of dissolution" (as Treitschke says about the Jews) because it spreads the seeds of eschatological freedom in an anxious, aggressive world.

V. MESSIANIC CHRISTOLOGY

Must Christian faith exclude the openness of the Jewish Messiah figure to the greater kingdom of God if it speaks messianically of Jesus? If faith does this, it is not able to tolerate an open Jewish hope beside it.[17] If it does not do this, how can it then still hope in Jesus with certainty? Jesus has

the personal attributes of being unexchangeable and unforgettable, and these are precisely the attributes which the Jewish picture of the Messiah, because of its very nature, cannot accord to him. For in this picture all of the Messiah's personal qualities can only be viewed abstractly because they are not yet based on the experience of him as a living person.[18]

But does Jesus really have these attributes? His "form" destroys precisely the yearning for a fixed form of hope. "He had no form or comeliness. As one from whom men hide their faces he was despised, and we esteemed him not," as the Gospels say with Isa. 53:2, 3. His person is defined by his destiny: "Crucified and raised," as the oldest confessions say. From this perspective he certainly remains unexchangeable and unforgettable, but the "experience of him as a living person" is at the same time a "mortifying" one. The "double end of his life" (Martin Kähler) reveals eschatological transcendence. He cannot be tied down to an image but rather liberates us from the idols of our present experience as well as of hope in the coming God. Christology therefore cannot be the elimination of messianic eschatology. Such an enthusiasm of fulfillment has again and again divinized Jesus and sought to quench the Jewish unrest.

Christology must rather lead to open eschatological hope. Cross and resurrection characterize present and future in the anticipatory act of God. Whoever engages in enthusiastic anticipation, whether it be in "having the Torah" or in the ecstatic triumph of the Christian religion, forfeits the present together with the future.

An eschatology which has a Christian foundation must therefore set out from an eschatologically open Christology.[19] Christianity can understand Jesus as the fulfilling confirmation of the messianic hope only if it indeed discovers within this person the messianic future of God himself. Only if it uncovers the difference and the bridge between the lordship of the Son of man and the lordship of God himself can it recognize its own eschatological provisionality. The Pauline notion that the Son will hand over the lordship to the Father so that God will be "all in all" (1 Cor. 15:28) points in this direction on the theological level. If this is taken seriously, Christian absolutism ceases. The church recognizes itself in provisional finality, hoping with the Jews and for the poor in the fulfillment of the kingdom in the history of God.

VI.   THE SUFFERING OF THE HOPING AND THE HOPE OF THE SUFFERING ONES

I have dealt with the question of Jesus' messiahship so extensively because without a revision in the christological foundations of Christianity there can scarcely be a new convergence of Jewish and Christian hope. The Jewish criticism which we have taken up here correctly applies to many historical formations in Christianity. But today we recognize that these historical forms of spiritualization and individualization of salvation as well as the triumphalistic-clerical divinization of Jesus cannot justfiably persist in view of his cross. The Jewish critique should lead Christianity to a deeper and better understanding of Jesus, his mission, his suffering, and his future. But this means that the concrete existence of the Jews constantly raises the question of the messianic hope in Christianity. The existence of the Jews again and again forces Christians to the knowledge that they are not yet at the goal, that their church is itself not the goal, but that with eschatological provisionality and brotherly openness they remain on the way.

Franz Rosenzweig was right when he said that the deepest reason for Christianity's hatred of Jews lay in its self-hatred, "in the hatred for its own unfulfillment, for its own not-yet."[20] Ecclesiastical and political persecution of the Jews in Christian societies is always directed against the unstillable Jewish hope in the Messiah in view of the unredeemedness of the world. A church or a

Christian society which passed off Jesus as the fulfillment of all human hope, thus liquidating the Jewish hope for the Messiah, and understood itself as the fully present kingdom of God on earth had to project its own disappointments onto the Jews. Even during the nineteenth-century emancipation of the Jews Schleiermacher's position demanded the surrender of their hope in the Messiah as the price of admission into the Christian-bourgeois society. But the more Christianity gets rid of its clerical and political enthusiasm of fulfillment and itself assumes the Son of man's form as an alien in this world, the more it will live with the messianic hope and accept the constant not-yet of Jewish messianic hope. Enthusiasm of presumed fulfillment without acceptance of the cross was the fatal flaw of the Christian triumphalism in the past. Resignation and the forfeiture of hope are the results of such presumption. After the expected loss of security in Christian states, the fermenting traditions of salvation history in Christianity have allied the hope of Christianity with Israel. The founding of the state of Israel also has a double effect: simultaneously fulfilling and negating.

The vitality of the messianic hope in Christianity will basically depend upon stressing the suffering form of Jesus and his community with the outcasts. Gershom Scholem has related a "truly staggering 'rabbinic fable' . . . from the second century" according to which the Messiah is transplanted "to the gates of Rome, where he dwells among the lepers and beggars of the Eternal City." "This symbolic antithesis between the true Messiah sitting at the gates of Rome and the head of Christendom, who reigns there, accompanies Jewish Messianic thought through the centuries."[21] Should not those who "on behalf of Christ" are beseeching others to reconciliation (2 Cor. 5:20) be found one day among those whom the Son of man called the least of his brothers (Matthew 25) and whom he blessed? Jews and Christians ultimately have their commonly given but variously experienced messianic hope not for themselves but for all of forsaken humanity. The Messiah arrives then neither in Jerusalem nor in Rome nor Geneva. He comes among the poor, the mourning, those who hunger for righteousness and are therefore persecuted. He comes among the "beggars and the lepers" in Jerusalem, Rome, and Geneva and other places.

Only when the suffering of those who hope messianically becomes the hope of those who are suffering in this world will Jews and Christians comprehend their provisional finality and give honor to the Messiah of the Godforsaken humanity.

NOTES TO CHAPTER FIVE

1. Sigmund Mowinkel, *He That Cometh: The Messianic Concept in the Old Testament and Latter Judaism* (New York: Oxford, 1956). Gershom Scholem, *The Messianic Idea in Judaism* (New York: Schocken Books, 1971), pp. 1–36.
2. S. Rudolph Bultmann, *Glauben und Verstehen*, II (1952), p. 246. Philipp Vielhauer, *Aufsätze zum Neuen Testament* (Munich: Chr. Kaiser, 1965), pp. 55 ff., and others.
3. Philipp Vielhauer, "Jesus und der Menschensohn," in *Aufsätze zum Neuen Testament*, pp. 92 ff., J. M. Schmidt, *Die Jüdische Apocalyptik* (Neukirchen: Neukirchner Verlag, 1969).
4. Cf. the traditional formula received by Paul, Rom. 1:3, and Scholem, *Messianic Idea*, pp. 10 ff.
5. Peter Stuhlmacher, *Gerechtigkeit Gottes bei Paulus* (Göttingen: Vandenhoeck & Ruprecht, 1965), p. 232, points out this context also for Paul.
6. Hans Joachim Iwand, *Die Gegenwart des Kommenden* (Munich: Chr. Kaiser, 1957).
7. Schalom Ben-Chorin, *Die Antwort des Jona* (Stuttgart: Evangelische Verlag, 1956), p. 99.
8. Scholem, *Messianic Idea*, p. 1. Franz Rosenzweig, *The Star of Redemption* (New York: Holt, Rinehart and Winston, 1971), part III.
9. Rudolf Bultmann, *History and Eschatology* (New York: Harper Torchbooks, 1957), demonstrates this and is himself an example of it. Scholem, *Messianic Idea*, p. 35, is right: "One may say, perhaps, the Messianic idea is the real anti-existentialist idea."
10. Scholem, *Messianic Idea*, p. 1.
11. Schalom Ben-Chorin, *Antwort*, p. 5.
12. Scholem, *Messianic Idea*, pp. 12 ff.
13. Margaret Susman, *Das Buch Hiob und das Schicksal des jüdische Volkes*, 2d ed. (Freiburg: Herder, 1948).
14. Jürgen Moltmann, *The Crucified God* (New York: Harper & Row, 1974).
15. Scholem, *Messianic Idea*, p. 11 quoted according to the *Midrash Tehillim* to Ps. 45:3.
16. So rightly Ernst Bloch, *Verfremdungen*, I, p. 219.
17. Cf. the novel of A. Schwarz-Bart, *Der Letzte der Gerechten* (Frankfurt: Fischer, 1960). English translation by Stephen Becker, *The Last of the Just* (New York: Bantam Books, 1961).
18. Scholem, *Messianic Idea*, pp. 15–16.
19. Jürgen Moltmann, *Theology of Hope*, trans. by James W. Leitch (New York: Harper & Row, 1967).
20. Rosenzweig, *Star of Redemption*, p. 413 (translation altered).
21. Scholem, *Messianic Idea*, p. 12.

VI.

The Crucified God and the Apathetic Man

The controversy over the existence of God has recently made many people unsure of themselves. They feel as if they have lost their bearings between the slogans "God is dead" and "God cannot die." In the struggle for a credible church and a more human society, others have therefore simply bracketed out the question of God and forgotten about it. They have freed themselves from church and theology and have adopted other ideologies and methods to struggle for a better world.

Without a revolution in the concept of God, however, there will be no revolutionary faith. Without God's liberation from idolatrous images produced by anxiety and *hubris,* there will be no liberating theology. Man always unfolds his humanity in relation to the divinity of his God, and he experiences himself in relationship to what appears to him as the highest being. He directs his life toward a highest value. He decides who he is by his ultimate concerns. As Martin Luther said: "Where you put the trust of your heart, that in fact is your God." That holds true for the Christian faith just as for every secular faith.

Behind the political and social crisis of the church in modern society stands the christological crisis: From whom does the church really take its bearings? Who is Jesus Christ, really, for us today? In this identity-crisis of Christianity, the question of God lies hidden: Which God governs Christian existence—the one who was crucified or the idols of religion, class, race, and society? Without a new clarity in Christian faith itself, there will be no credibility in Christian life. It would be short-sighted to suppose that old theology connects easily to new praxis. The transformations which one seeks externally through protest movements, through communes, and through struggles for the liberation of the oppressed must come internally from the "hard core" of the Christian faith. More lies hidden there than has previously become visible in history. Where does the difference lie?

At the core of Christianity we find the history of the man from Nazareth. Through forgiveness of sins, liberating miracles, and signs of hope he proclaimed that the kingdom of God had come near to the poor, the sinner, the outcast, and the victims of discrimination. He entered into the way of suffering and was killed as a blasphemer, as a threat to national security, and, on the cross, as one abandoned by God. According to the witness of the Easter faith, this is the one whom God raised up. This is the one in whom the future of God and of man's freedom became flesh. At the core of Christianity we find, at the same time, the history of the God who humiliated himself, who became man, who took upon himself the suffering of inhumanity, and who died in the Godforsakenness of the cross.

I

Whether we are conservative or revolutionary, whether we are satisfied with our society or want to transform it, we all believe at bottom in action and success. We are convinced that we can solve all problems through right programs and actions. As Sidney Hook observes, Western society is an officially optimistic society.[1] The built-in values of our life and our system condemn us to activity, success, profit, and progress. If we experience failure, if we are frustrated, then we move on to another place, "where the action is." "What can, what must we do? What next?" Those are our only questions, for we hate to admit and reflect upon what misery our optimism and our programs of action have inflicted upon other persons and upon nature. The conservatives are proud of the successes which they and their fathers have brought to pass. The revolutionaries want to see different and new successes. They look for "God's activity in history" and want to be "where things are happening most dynamically."

Both stem from the same stock and sit in the same boat. Who is their God? He is the God of action, the strong God ever on the side of the stronger battalions, the God who wins battles and leads his own to victory. He is the idol of mankind's "history of success." This God is power, and only successful faith makes an impression. What follows from the divinity of this God for the humanity of life? Life then means only acting and producing, making and prevailing. This one-sided orientation toward action and success, however, makes men inhuman and represses the other weaker and more sensitive side of life. From this perspective, those who suffer are sick; those who weep and mourn show no stamina. The world has nothing more to say to us. It does not touch us. One can do with the world what one wants. No despair need tear at our hearts. We become hard in the give and take of life. The suffering of others makes no impression on us. Love is no longer a passion, but only a sexual act.

The man of success does not weep, and he keeps smiling only out of courtesy. Coldness is his style. That which his activity demands he calls "good"; that which hinders his success is "bad." The other man is simply his competitor in the struggle for existence. "Survival of the fittest" is his eschatology. Just as he wants to control the world, so also he holds himself under self-control. In short, he who believes in the God of action and success becomes an apathetic man. He takes no more notice of the world, of other men, or of his own emotions. He remains oblivious to the suffering his actions cause. He does not want to know about that and represses crucifying experiences from his life.

The God of success and the apathetic man of action completely contradict what we find at the core of Christianity: the suffering God and the loving, vulnerable man. On the other hand, the crucified God contradicts the God of success and his idol-worshipers all the more totally. He contradicts the officially optimistic society. He also contradicts the revolutionary activism of the sons of the old establishment. The severity of the cross contradicts the old and the new triumphal theology (*theologia gloria*) which we produce in the churches in order to keep pace with the transformations of an activistic and rapidly changing society.

We, too, find the memory of the crucified God discomforting. We gladly falsify it by changing the cross into an idol of our driving practical optimism in various crusades. As Douglas Hall has written: "The greatest misfortune would be if Christians used the

Theology of Hope as just another religious aid for avoiding the experience of the cross that many in our sector of the battlefield can no longer avoid."[2] In fact, there is no true *theology of hope* which is not first of all a *theology of the cross*. There will be no new hope for humanity, if it does not arise from the destruction of the apathetic "man of action" through a recognition of the suffering that he causes. Apathetic existence must be changed into its opposite: an existence of pathos leading to sympathy, sensitivity, and love. There will be no *Christian*, that is, no *liberating theology* without the life-giving memory of the suffering of God on the cross.

Over two hundred years ago, European society was already traveling the optimistic and erroneous path of active world improvement. For the Enlightenment period, the world of nature, principles, and ideas was a reflection of the power and glory of God. If man would only correspond morally to this glorious world of God, then the kingdom of God would be realized! Then in 1755 came the famous Lisbon earthquake, and optimism collapsed, reverting into pessimism and even nihilism.

The corresponding "earthquakes" of our time are not found in nature and physical evil, but rather in history and in inhuman evil. For my people, as executioners, and for the Jews, as victims, it is Auschwitz. As a German I do not have the right to say it, but for the American people, as executioners, and for the Vietnamese, as victims, it may be called Vietnam. For us who are white, rich, and dominant, it is the cry of the starving, oppressed, and racially victimized masses. For our technocratic society, it may become the silent death of nature, carrying us to destruction. At this point, too, our optimism collapses. What will take its place? Cynicism and apathy?

II

Allow me to become personal here for a moment. Ten years ago, I went through the remains of the concentration camp at Maidanek in Poland. With each step it became physically more difficult to go further and look at the thousands of children's shoes, clothing remnants, collected hair, and gold teeth. At that moment from shame I would have preferred to be swallowed up by the earth, if I had not believed: "God is with them. They will rise again." Later, I found in the visitors' book the inscriptions of others: "Never again can this be allowed to happen. We will fight to see that this never again comes to pass." I respect this answer, but it does not help the murdered ones. I also respect my own answer, which I gave at that time. But it is not sufficient.

How is faith in God, how is being human, possible after Auschwitz? I don't know. But it helps me to remember the story that Elie Wiesel reports in his book on Auschwitz called *Night*. Two Jewish men and a child were hanged. The prisoners were forced to watch. The men died quickly. The boy lived on in torture for a long while. "Then someone behind me said: 'Where is God?' and I was silent. After half an hour he cried out again: 'Where is God? Where is he?' And a voice in me answered: 'Where is God? . . . he hangs there from the gallows. . . .' "

A theology after Auschwitz would be impossible, were not the *sch'ma* Israel and the Lord's prayer prayed in Auschwitz itself, were not God himself in Auschwitz, suffering with the martyred and the murdered. Every other answer would be blasphemy. An absolute God would make us indifferent. The God of action and success would let us forget the dead, which we still cannot forget. God as Nothingness would make the entire world into the *univers concentrationaire*. Let me break off here, and now try, step by step, to penetrate into the mystery of God's suffering, attempting to show how the horizon of humanity exists in the situation of the crucified God.

III

The Apathetic God and Human Freedom

Apatheia, in the world of antiquity, is a metaphysical axiom and an ethical ideal which early Christianity unavoidably encountered.[3] Apathy combines the honoring of God's divinity and the striving for human liberation. It means remaining unaffected by external influences, a lack of sensitivity peculiar to dead objects, and a freedom of the spirit from needs and drives. In the physical sense, apathy means unchangeability; in the psychic sense, insensitivity; but in the ethical sense, freedom.

Since Plato and Aristotle, God's perfection has been designated as *apatheia*. God is good and cannot be the cause of evil. God is perfect and thus has no needs. God is sufficient and thus needs neither love nor hate. Nothing can befall him that would make him suffer. He knows neither wrath nor grace. God is totally free. Therefore, since Aristotle, it has been said: *theos apathes*. The wise man's moral ideal is to become similar to God and to share in his domain. The wise man must overcome his drives and needs and lead a life free from trouble and fear, from wrath and love, in short, an apathetic life.

Free from passions and interests, he recognizes the truth of ideas. Untouched by pain and happiness, nothing stirs him. He no longer feels what other men consider to be good or evil. He uses all earthly things indifferently, as if he did not have them. Thus he lives in happy resignation. We can see that here *apatheia* means the liberation of man from dependence upon nature.

This liberation succeeds only through a rigorous renunciation of everything bodily. Only by becoming free from oneself and learning to dominate oneself does one gain that freedom from nature possessed by God. Apathy here does not mean that sickness which appears today as lack of feeling and participation. It is rather the negative reverse-side of transcendent freedom from the material world. Intellect and will were therefore never reckoned among the passions. Even the apathetic God has always possessed intellect and will.

Ancient Judaism and ancient Christianity took over this ideal of apathy, and each in its own way filled it with new life. Philo portrayed Abraham as the model of *apatheia*. As Abraham became obedient to God, he withdrew from the world of drives and needs. Yet the God of Philo was, of course, different from the God of Aristotle. Hence Abraham filled the ideal of *apatheia* with a kind of life other than, say, a Stoic. The church fathers took over the philosophical concept of the apathetic God, calling God's intellect "the Son" and God's will "the Holy Spirit." For them the apathetic and free God was the God of love (*agape*). Because true love arises out of freedom from self-seeking and anxiety, and because it loves *sine ira et studio,* one understood apathy as the presupposition for *agape*.

Jews and Christians thus took up the apathetic theology of antiquity as preparation for their own positive theology. As history shows, however, they both ran into serious difficulties. The Old Testament speaks often of the wrath of God. But if the apathetic God neither loves nor hates, how can he then be wrathful? How can he be interested in the history of his people on earth? How can he have compassion on Israel's suffering? The New Testament tells, in essence, the passion story of Jesus Christ. But how can the Son of God suffer? How can he change? How can he love and feel pain? How can he die on the cross abandoned by God?

The passion story did not correspond to the ideals of Stoicism. One either had to break through the axiom of apathy or to reinterpret the passion story. Neither of these alternatives was taken up, however, and therefore we still stand today before the unsolved problem of the suffering God.

There are various God-situations in which man finds himself and various ways in which he experiences himself and leads his life. The God-situation of *apatheia* leads man into transcendent freedom from his body and environment. Faith in the apathetic God leads to the ethics of man's liberation from need and drive, and to dominion over body and nature.

However the God-situation in which Israel discovers itself as God's people is different. It is the situation of the pathos of God and the sympathy of man. The God-situation in which Christians discover themselves as Christians is once again different. It is the situation of the incarnate, crucified God and the loving man.

The Pathos of God and the Sympathy of Man

It was Rabbi Abraham Heschel, who, in his Berlin dissertation of 1936 and later in his book *The Prophets* (1963), first named the theology of the prophets a theology of pathos. Significantly, he attained this insight through a critical consideration of the ancient tradition in medieval Judaism. The prophets did not have a new idea of God, but rather understood themselves and the people of Israel in that God-situation which Heschel calls God's pathos. In pathos, the all-powerful God goes outside of himself and enters into in a relationship with a people of his choosing. He places his complete interest in his covenant with his people. Hence he is affected by the experiences, actions, and suffering of Israel.

His pathos has nothing to do with the whims of the mythical

gods. It is his free relationship to creation, to people, and to history. God takes man seriously to the point that he suffers from the actions of man and can be injured through them. The prophets did not identify God's pathos with his essence, but rather saw in pathos the form of his relationship to the world, of his involvement and concern.

Prophecy is therefore not the foretelling of the future, as determined by fate or by God's plan of salvation. It is rather an insight into the present pathos of God, in suffering at Israel's disobedience, and in passion for justice and honor in the world. When Spinoza maintained that God neither loves nor scorns, he completely failed to recognize the pathos of God. God's wrath is nothing less than his wounded love and a pain which cuts to the heart. His wrath is therefore an expression of enduring interest in man. Only indifference would be a withdrawal of God from pathos for man.

What follows for man from this God-situation? In the sphere of the apathetic God, man becomes *homo apathetikos*. In the situation of God's pathos, however, he becomes *homo sympathetikos*. Sympathy is the openness of a person for the presence of another (Max Scheler). It has a dialogical structure. The divine pathos finds its resonance in the sympathy of man, in his openness and sensitivity to the divine, the human, and the natural.

Through sympathy, man corresponds to the pathos of God. He does not come into an ahistorical *unio mystica,* but rather into historical *unio sympathetica* with God. He is angry with God's wrath. He loves with God's love. He suffers with God's suffering. He hopes with God's hope. In covenant with the God of pathos, man steps outside of himself, takes part in the life of others, and can rejoice and suffer with them. He is interested and concerned.

This sympathy is freedom, too. It is not a world-transcending freedom of the mind, but a life-awakening freedom of the heart, that is, of the whole man. It is not the freedom of rulers over nature and body, but the freedom of brothers in their solidarity.

Heschel developed his theology of divine pathos as a bipolar theology of the covenant. God is free in himself, yet at the same time involved in the covenant. From this a second bipolarity emerges. The sympathy of man responds to the pathos of God. The prophet is an *isch-haruach,* a man driven by the Spirit of God.

Through man's sympathy, the Spirit thus answers to God's pathos. This indicates a dual personality in God.

These thoughts may be extended further if we consider the theology of God's self-humiliation as developed by the rabbis of the first century.[4] They took Ps. 18:36 (according to the King James Version: "and thy gentleness hath made me great"; according to Luther: "when you humiliate me, you make me great") and translated it like this: "You show to me your greatness through your self-humiliation." The history of God's self-humiliation begins with the creation and reaches to the end. God is present in two ways; he dwells in heaven and also among the humiliated. He is exalted yet cares for those who are humbled. He is the God of Gods yet creates justice for widows and orphans. Like a servant, he bears a flame before Israel in the desert. Like a father, he bears his people with its sin. Thus he encounters the limited, the humble, and the least of humanity. These are the accommodations of God to human history.

At the same time, these are the anticipations of his universal indwelling in glory at the end of days. Yet God not only humiliates himself to enter into the situation of his finite creature. He also enters into the situation of the guilty creature. His sorrow over Israel shows that God himself suffers with the suffering of Israel. In his dwelling (*sheckhina*) with the people, he suffers with the people, goes with them into exile, and feels affliction with martyrs.

Conversely, it can be said, therefore, that God saves himself when he saves Israel. Because he has bound his name with Israel, Israel will then be saved when God glorifies himself. The suffering of God is the means through which Israel is saved. God himself is the "ransom" for Israel. In the rabbinic theology of the first century, a theology of the cross is in fact implicit. The God who suffers in exile with Israel preserves the people from despair and fear. The realization of God's fellow-suffering impedes apathy, maintains sympathy for God in life, and holds hope for the future of God open.

In this rabbinic theology, one also finds the perception of the suffering of God linked to the thought of God's dual personality. God does not suffer with the people only externally in persecution. Suffering exists within the God who has the ends of the earth in his hands and the Spirit who dwells with suffering Israel. God is not only there in suffering; the suffering is also in God himself. It exists between God and God. God is not only involved in history; history is also in God himself. Therefore, it can be said: In suffering, I flee from God to God.

The Crucified God and the Loving Man

Christian faith does not have a new idea of God, but rather finds itself in a different God-situation. It is defined through the passion of God and the cross of Christ. It is related to the Jewish God-situation, for the pathos of God in the Old Testament is the presupposition for the passion of God according to the New Testament. Where does the difference lie?

The prophetic theology of pathos proceeded from God's covenant with his people and, on this basis, developed a bipolar theology between the pathos of God and the sympathy of the Spirit in man. However, those who discern the God-situation in the crucified one are men from among all peoples. While for Israel the immediacy of God exists in the covenant, for Christians there is Christ himself, who mediates the fatherhood of God and the power of the Spirit. Christian theology cannot develop (as is often done in process theology) a bipolar theology of interaction between God and the Spirit in man. It must, for the sake of the crucified one, intentionally become a *trinitarian theology*. Through the crucified one, that dialogical God-relationship is first opened up. Through Christ, God himself creates the conditions necessary to enter upon a relationship of pathos and sympathy. Through the crucified one, he creates a new covenant for those who cannot meet these conditions because they are Godless and Godforsaken.

A direct relationship between God and man severed from the person and history of Christ would be inconceivable from a Christian standpoint. Only the recognition of God in Christ, and above all in the crucified one, makes possible the dialogical life in the Spirit, in sympathy, and in hope for those who are "on the outside." If God was in Christ, as Paul says, then through Christ a new God-situation becomes manifest. But how does this divine context look, as revealed in the cross, and how does man experience himself within it?

According to Philippians 2, Christian theology speaks of God's ultimate and complete self-humiliation in the person and crucifixion of Jesus. God thereby enters into the limited, finite situation of man. He not only has dealings with it, but also embraces it and makes it into a part of his own life.

He does not become Spirit, so that man would have to ascend into the Spirit to find God. He does not become simply the covenant-partner of an elect people, so that one would have to belong to this people to experience community with him. He humbles himself and assumes the whole and complete being of man, so that everyone can share in him through his human experience.

If God's humiliation completes itself in the cross of Christ, then God not only enters into the finitude of man but also into the situation of his God-abandonedness.

In Jesus, God does not die a natural death, but rather the violent death of a condemned person on the cross. At Golgatha he dies the death of complete God-abandonedness. The suffering in the suffering of Jesus is the abandonment, and indeed condemnation, by the God whom he called Father. According to Mark 15:34, Jesus dies with the cry, "My God, my God, why hast thou forsaken me?" The heathen centurion then answers: "Truly this man was the Son of God." The confession of Jesus' divine sonship in Mark, which comes in the wake of Jesus' Godforsakenness, is articulated, paradoxically, by a heathen. He did not see a divine hero and helper of humanity. He did not see merely an innocent sufferer on the cross. He heard Jesus' cry of Godforsakenness in rejection by God, and believed. The Godforsaken Son of God takes the eternal death of the forsaken and the damned upon himself in order to become God of the forsaken and brother of the damned. Every person damned and forsaken by God can, in the crucified one, experience community with God. The incarnate God is present and accessible to the humanity of every man. No one needs to play a role or to transform himself in order to come to his humanity through Christ.

Through the abandonment of one, the crucified God is near to everyone. He imparts no loneliness and no rejection which he had not taken upon himself in Jesus' death. Therefore, neither self-justification nor self-accusation is necessary before him. Nothing more exists that could exclude the lost man from the situation of the pain of the Father, the love of the Son, and the life of the Spirit. Without limits and without conditions, unhappy man is received into full community with God. In the cross of Christ, God took absolute death upon himself in order to give his infinite life to man condemned to death.

To recognize the new God-situation in the cross of Christ, however, also means to recognize that the cross, our inescapable suffering, and our hopeless despair exist in God. A theology of the cross must in this way become part of a trinitarian theology, or else it cannot take up the problem of suffering. It is good but not sufficient to say that God is "the fellow-sufferer who understands" (Whitehead).[5]

God not only participates in our suffering but also makes our suffering into his own, and takes our death into his life. Paul, therefore, accepted the word for "abandon"—*paradidonai*—and reinterpreted it into an expression for love. "He who spared not his own Son, but *gave him up* for us all. . . ." (Rom. 8:32). In the historical abandonment of Jesus on the cross, Paul sees the divine sacrifice of the Son. By stressing that it was God's "own" Son, Paul indicates that the sacrifice and suffering of Christ also affect the Father himself, yet not in the same ways as the Son.

Jesus suffers dying in forsakenness, but he does not suffer death because death itself is not something one can "suffer." The Father, however, in the pain of his love, suffers the death of his son. Kazoh Kitamori has aptly described this as the "pain of God."[6] Because the dying of the Son is something other than the pain of the Father, one cannot speak absolutely of God's death as occurs in the God-is-dead theology. To understand the suffering and the death in God, one must speak in trinitarian terms and must set aside the simple monotheistic concept of God.

In the cross of Christ, a rupture tears, as it were, through God himself. It does not simply tear through Christ, as the doctrine of the two natures states. At first it sounds paradoxical if one says that God himself is abandoned by God. God rejects himself. God cries out to God. Or, as Luther said: "There God dies to God." This paradox is resolved, however, if, with regard to the cross, one learns to make trinitarian distinctions within God himself. The event at the cross is an event within God. It is an event between the sacrificing Father and the abandoned Son in a power of sacrifice that deserves to be named the Spirit. In the cross, Jesus and the Father are in the deepest sense separated in forsakenness, yet are at the same time most inwardly united through the Spirit of sacrifice. From the event between Jesus and his Father at the cross, the Spirit goes forth which upholds the abandoned, justifies the despised, and will bring the dead to life.

If we understand the doctrine of the Trinity as a description of the God-situation in the cross of Christ then it is no longer speculation. It is nothing less than a summary of the passion story. The material principle of the doctrine of the Trinity is the cross. The formal principle of the theology of the cross is the doctrine of the Trinity. We then understand the *homousios* in historical terms. It is not God's essence behind or beyond history but God's history in the Christ-event. And if all historical misery is taken up in the cross of Christ God's history can be called "the history of history." The person who wants to say who God is must therefore tell the passion story of Christ as the story of God.

IV

What characterizes the new life-space of men which is opened up by the God-situation in the cross of Christ? What does recognition of the "crucified God" mean for the history of the world's suffering?

Whoever suffers without reason always feels at first that he is forsaken by God and all good things. Whoever cries to God in this suffering however joins fundamentally in the death-cry of Jesus. But then for him God is not only a hidden object to whom he cries; in a very personal sense he is rather the human God who cries with him and in him and who intercedes for him where he in his misery grows silent. The suffering person thus enters into the full situation of God. He cries with the abandoned Son to the Father, and the Spirit intercedes for him with groanings.

How is this to be understood? The person who suffers does not only protest against his fate. Indeed, he suffers because he lives, and he is full of life because he has an interest in life and because he loves. He who no longer loves becomes apathetic and no longer even suffers. Life and death are for him a matter of indifference. The more one loves, however, the more vulnerable one becomes. The more one becomes capable of suffering, the more one becomes capable of happiness. The reverse is also true. The more one is capable of joy, the greater one's capacity for sorrow. This could be called the dialectic of human life. Love gives vitality to living, but it also makes man mortal. The vitality of life and the deadlines of death are experienced at one and the same time through that interest in life we call love.

But how can man, despite disappointment, suffering, and dying, remain in love? The God of theism is poor. He cannot suffer because he cannot love. Whoever believes in him becomes apathetic. The protesting atheist loves in a desperate way. He suffers because he loves, yet he protests against suffering and against love, and easily becomes hardened. Like Ivan Karamazov, he wants to give back his admission ticket to life.

Faith that originates from the God-situation at the cross does not answer the question of suffering with a religious explanation of "why everything must be exactly as it is," so that one simply submits to it. But neither does it harden into the mere gesture of protest which says that "everything as it is, is impermissible." Rather, it leads protesting love back to its origin: "He who remains in love, remains in God and God in him" (1 Jn. 4:17).

Where people suffer because they love, God suffers in them and they suffer in God. Where this God suffers the death of Jesus and thereby demonstrates the power of his love, there people also find the power to remain in love despite pain and death, becoming neither bitter nor superficial. They gain the power of affliction and can hold fast to the dead.

He who enters into love, and through love experiences the deadliness of death, enters also into the "history of God." On the other hand, he who recognizes the trinitarian history of God in the cross of Christ can live with the terrors of history and despite them remain in love. Through complete worldliness of living (Dietrich Bonhoeffer), through which he suffers and becomes guilty in solidarity with mankind, he lives in *God*. As Hegel said so aptly: "Not the life which shrinks back from death and preserves itself completely from destruction, but the life which endures death and, in the midst of death, perseveres—that is the life of the Spirit."[7]

V

In conclusion, let me come back to the beginning. Our officially optimistic society believes in the idols of action and success. Through their compulsive inhumanity, they lead many persons into apathy and despair. The churches in this society often function as nothing more than religious establishments, caretakers for the idols and laws of this society. If this society is to turn itself toward humanity, the churches must become Christian. They must destroy the idols of action and apathy, of success and anxiety; proclaim the human, the suffering, the crucified God; and learn to live in his situation. They must discover the meaning of suffering and sorrow, and spread abroad the spirit of compassion, sympathy, and love. They must confront successful and despairing man with the truth of the cross in his situation, so that man may become a compassionate, joyous, and thereby free being.

Without a revolution in the concept of God, there is no revolutionary theology. Without liberation of the crucified God from the idols of power, there is no liberating theology! God is not dead; God is not a revolutionary activist. He hangs there from the cross of his love and glorifies his sacrifice through resurrection. The misery that we cause and the unhappiness that we experience are his misery and unhappiness. Our history of suffering is taken up into his history of suffering. In that way, his future becomes our future, and the happiness of his love is the resurrection of our life.

To recognize God in the crucified Christ means to grasp the trinitarian history of God and to understand oneself and this whole world with Auschwitz and Vietnam, with race hatred and hunger, as existing in the history of God. God is not dead. Death is in God. God suffers by us. He suffers with us. Suffering is in God. God does not ultimately reject, nor is he ultimately rejected. Rejection is within God. In the way hidden in the cross, the triune God is already on the way toward becoming "all in all," and "in him we live and move and have our being." When he brings his history to completion (1 Cor. 15:28), his suffering will be transformed into joy, and thereby our suffering as well.

NOTES TO CHAPTER SIX

1. Sidney Hook in Robert L. Heilbroner, *The Future as History* (New York, Harper & Row, 1960).
2. Douglas J. Hall, "The Theology of Hope in an Officially Optimistic Society," *Religion in Life*, 40 (1971): 390.
3. The most important progress in Christian theology today is being made in overcoming the "apathy" axiom in theology. It is a truly ecumenical undertaking because Catholic and Protestant theologians are working together on it. Cf. Karl Rahner, "Bemerkungen zum Traktat 'de Trinitate,' " *Schriften zur Theologie*, IV, 1964; Hans Urs von Balthasar, "Mysterium Paschale," in *Mysterium Salutis, Grundriss heilsgeschtlicher Dogmatik*, III, 2, 1969; Heribert Mühlen, *Die Verändlichkeit Gottes als Horizont einer zukünftigen Christologie*, 1969; Hans Küng, *Menschwerdung Gottes*, 1970; similarly on the Protestant side, Karl Barth, *Kirchliche Dogmatik*, II, and IV, 1-4; Paul Althaus, *Theologische Aufsätze*, 1929; Eberhard Jüngel, *Gottes Sein ist im Werden*, 1965; Rudolf Weth, "Heil im gekreuzigten Gott," *Evangelische Theologie*, 31 (1971).
4. Peter Kuhn, *Gottes Selbsterniedrigung in der Theologie der Rabbinen* (Munich: 1968).
5. Alfred North Whitehead, *Process and Reality: An Essay in Cosmology* (New York: Macmillan, 1967), p. 532. Cf. Daniel Day Williams, "Suffering and Being in Empirical Theology," in *The Future of Empirical Theology*, ed. Bernard E. Meland (Chicago: University of Chicago Press, 1969), pp. 175–194. I agree with Professor Williams on the matter, but do not believe that the cosmological conception of God (God's primordial and consequent nature) sufficiently grasps the problem of suffering. On the other hand, the starting point for a trinitarian theology of the cross can take up process-theology ideas of the suffering God and use them for a Christian cosmology. Even the cosmos itself groans in travail (Romans 8), and even its suffering has become through Christ a part of the suffering of God.
6. Kazoh Kitamori, *The Pain of God* (Richmond: John Knox, 1965).
7. G. W. F. Hegel, *Phänomenologie des Geistes*, Introduction, p. 30.

VII.

Dostoevsky and
the Hope of Prisoners

I am not a specialist in Russian literature, nor am I a Dostoevskyan scholar. I have never been to Russia and I do not speak Russian. I am only a reader and admirer of Dostoevsky. But for more than three years I was in a prisoner-of-war camp and I understand something of the language of prisoners, the loneliness and the dreams of the "unhappy." I first read *The House of the Dead, Crime and Punishment,* and *The Possessed* in the barracks behind barbed wire. Dostoevsky helped me to understand myself and my situation which was "full of dreams and faces." He showed me how to suffer and to hope in and with the people. If I remember rightly, it was during that time among the prisoners that the motifs of the "theology of hope" came into being.

These impulses did not grow out of the yearning to be released and finally to "go home." Rather hope came to life as the prisoner accepted his imprisonment, affirmed the barbed wire, and in this situation discovered the real human being in himself and others. It was not at his release but even while in prison that the "resurrection from the dead" happened for him. Faith inside the "house of the dead" is resurrection faith, as Dostoevsky continually emphasizes. And so I maintained later in *Theology of Hope*: Christian faith is resurrection faith or it is not yet Christian faith. This is not a dogmatic issue but is evident for the prisoners in the "house of the dead." If the "dead" and the "buried alive" are to have faith in God what else can it be but resurrection faith? What else can be the faith of sinners, who after all are the "unhappy," the "suffering," except forgiveness, reconciliation, and love? What can be the faith of the "humiliated and the insulted" other than liberation? In the good society such a man seems like an "idiot" and such a "resurrection" seems like the "dream of a ridiculous man." But the prostitutes and the murderers, the passionate ones (*Leidenschaftlichen*) and the suffering ones (*Leidenden*) understand him and his experience.

Dostoevsky is at once fascinating and strange. He is a psychologist, in whose presence one feels oneself penetrated to the very depths, so that one might exclaim as does Stravrogin to Tihon: "cursed psychologist!" But Dostoevsky is more than merely a penetrating psychologist. He is in the broadest sense religious. Berdyaev called him a "pneumatologist." He called himself a "higher realist." He was a materialistic idealist, a materialist with a dream of the future and a mysticism of the wholly other. The figures of his novels are psychologically impossible. As he depicted it, Russia never existed. But in an all-too-human reality he saw those ideas and sparks, "seeds," as it were, which God "took from the beyond and threw upon earth so that his earthly garden would bloom." This is Platonic, and yet it says more than Plato. "It is beauty which will save the world," he once said. And so in a paradoxical way he made visible this transcendent beauty in the grieving, hateful, distorted, and despairing faces of his characters. Thus we experience them as terribly eccentric: they point to something beyond themselves. They are living protests, question marks, and beckonings for the transfiguration of the whole world. Beauty is grace, and no one shows this gracefulness better than the prostitute Sonia in her love for the murderer Raskolnikov. In the suffering of the criminal, in the compassion which knows no limits and no disgust, in the "brotherhood of all men" which Dostoevsky affirmed in his Pushkin speech in Moscow, this transfiguration of the world appears in the medium of the novelist's art. Everyone is guilty for everything. No one will be saved unless all are saved. Common suffering and solidarity in the negatives will liberate the world, will make it a human world and therefore God's world.

We constantly encounter these paradoxes in Dostoevsky. He is read and understood in historical periods of extreme contradictions. Interest in him arises in times of internal and external social collapse. As the Dostoevskyan literary criticism indicates, such a period broke onto the scene in Western Europe after the First World War. The books by Nicholas Berdyaev, Eduard Thurney-

sen, Vyacheslav Iwanov, Stefan Zweig, and André Gide led many
people in Germany to Dostoevsky. They recognized the untruth,
the inhumanity, and the vain activity of their society because they
were encountered by the truth of men who were exploited, misused, and hounded to death. The influence of Dostoevsky was
again felt keenly in Western Europe just after the Second World
War through the books of Steinbüchel, Fyodor Stepun, M. Doerne,
Romano Guardini, and others. Those who returned from the concentration camps, the prisoner-of-war camps, and the ruins understood him.

Then, as industrialism dominated the external and Existentia-
lism the internal scene, Dostoevsky's influence in Europe and
America waned. As the established society reacted with increasing
anxiety and rigidity to the protesting students' rediscovery of
socialism and to the rise of left and right sectarian groups, Dostoevsky was forgotten.

I believe that we are standing before a new "hour of Dostoevsky," for many people are becoming inwardly disappointed over
short-lived protests and mere technocratic reforms. They are struck
by the ultimate questions and are sensing that the answers may
be in religious dimensions. Hopefully, they will find a religion
that will carry on the revolution of man for which they were
yearning.

The "hour of Dostoevsky" can also break into the Soviet Union
so that the unfinished, unrealized hopes of the 1917 revolution of
the Russian people may be renewed. Such a beginning was made
six years ago with the famous Kafka discussion in the Czechoslovakia which nurtured "socialism with a human face." Dostoevsky
can again become the voice of the silent ones in the underground.

In this context I would like to speak of three truths which I
have found in Dostoevsky: (1) the imprisonment of man, (2) the
resurrection of the dead, and (3) messianism.

"Man is not at home with himself, but is, as it were, on a visit."
Already prior to his own arrest and his years in Katorga, Dostoevsky conceived of *being imprisoned* as a basic human situation. He
later pictured this situation as the "dog house," the "cellar clink,"
or the "coffin" of Raskolnikov's confining student room. But then
this became his own experience and in his own experience his

vision of the true man. He described it in *The House of the Dead.*[1]
How does the prisoner become a free man? "Our prison stood at
the edge of the fortress grounds, close to the fortress wall. One
would sometimes, through a chink in the fence, take a peep into
God's world. . . . Outside the gate is the world of light and freedom. . . . But those living on this side of the fence picture that
world as some unattainable fairyland." *The prisoner is a great
dreamer.*

"That is why every convict in Russia, whatever prison he may
be in, grows restless in the spring with the first kindly rays of sun-
shine. Though by no means everyone intends to run away . . yet
they dream at least of how they might escape and where they might
escape to and comfort their hearts with the very desire, with the
very imagination of its being possible."

"To change one's luck" is the technical expression. "Every fugi-
tive looks forward, not exactly to complete freedom—he knows
that is almost impossible—but either to getting into another institution or being sent as a settler, or being tried again for a fresh
offense committed when he was tramping; in fact he does not care
what becomes of him, so long as he is not sent back to the old place
he is sick of, his former prison."

"One glimpses a bird in the limpid blue air and for a long time
one watches its flight: now it darts over the water, now it vanishes
in the blue depths, now it reappears again, a speck flitting in the
distance." The freedom of the bird entrances the fettered one and
makes him blind and oblivious to his surroundings.

"During that first year I failed to notice many things in my
misery. I shut my eyes and did not want to look. Among my spite-
ful and hostile companions in prison, I did not observe the good
ones—the men who were capable of thought and feeling in spite
of the repellent outer husk. In the midst of ill-natured sayings, I
sometimes failed to notice kind and friendly words. . . ."

"To change one's luck" is the dream of the prisoner and if an
escape actually succeeded, "something like hope, daring, the possibility of 'changing their luck' stirred in every soul. . . . And at
this thought everyone plucked up his spirit and looked defiantly
at his mates. At any rate, they all seemed suddenly proud and
began looking condescendingly at the sergeants."

For some time there lived in the prison also an eagle, one of the small eagles of the steppes. He had been brought into the prison wounded and exhausted. The prisoners loved him but he was "mistrustful and hostile to all." "To be sure, he is a free, fierce bird; you can't get him used to prison," they said. Finally they carried him out of the prison. "Strange to say, they all seemed pleased, as though they too had won a share of freedom." Without looking around, the eagle hobbled into the steppe, fluttering his healthy wing. "And he doesn't look round; he hasn't looked round once," said one bitterly, "Ah, to be sure it's freedom. It's freedom he sniffs." "You can't see him now, mates. . . . What are you standing there for?" shouted the guards. This untamable eagle with a wounded wing is indeed the starkest image of the forsaken prisoner hungering for freedom. *Imprisonment* and *hope*: and the one only intensifies the other.

"Totally without hope one cannot live." Without some goal and some effort to reach it no man can live. When he has lost all hope and object in life, man often becomes a monster in his misery." To live without hope is to cease to live. Hell is hopelessness. It is no accident that above the entrance to Dante's hell is the inscription: "Leave behind all hope, you who enter here." I have seen imprisoned men whose last hopes vanished. They lay down, became sick, and died. If there is today in our society a sickness of youth, though by no means limited to youth, it is this sickness of objective and goal. The future becomes dark. It is the cold despair in which "nothing really matters" to a person and he or she succumbs to the death wish. *Acedia, tristesse,* or melancholy in the Middle Ages was considered one of the deadly sins against the Spirit. "It is not so much sin which plunges us into calamity but rather despair," said Chrysostom. Is this not the sickness of a society which increasingly eliminates human chances because of its cycle of work and profit, control and bureaucracy? Whoever takes away hope from a person or a society kills them. Dostoevsky gained an uncommonly clear recognition of this in prison.

On the other hand, however, hope makes one restless. One can no longer put up with one's situation. Every fatherland becomes a foreign country, every house a prison. "I have mentioned already," he said, "that all the convicts lived in prison not as though they were at home there, but as though they were at a hotel, on a journey, at some temporary halt. Even men sentenced for their whole life were restless or miserable, and no doubt every one of them was dreaming of something almost impossible. This everlasting uneasiness, which showed itself unmisakably, though not in words, this strange impatient and intense hope . . . this dreaminess gave the greater number of the prisoners a gloomy and sullen, almost abnormal, expression." Thus hope, as the dream of freedom, becomes the worst persecutor of the prisoners. It relentlessly makes them aware of their intolerable situation. It turns their suffering into pain and their imprisonment into agony. Today we often experience precisely this negative effect of hope.

The two mutually stimulate each other: *imprisonment* would be unbearable without hope. Without hope one cannot live, and this is true not only in prison. But *hope* is that which makes the prisoner gloomy, unsociable, and bitter. Not even the little bit of life which is left to him can have the atmosphere of a house and a home. The prisoner must hope in order to survive, but hope is what really makes him a prisoner, letting him know that he is imprisoned. This is the situation of the convicts in the "house of the dead." For Dostoevsky it is the revelation of the true situation of man in general.

Yet there is still a third element present in the agonizing situation between imprisonment and hope. Dostoevsky calls our attention to it: *The prisoner is a free man.*[2] Indeed he is not the "criminal," as he was hated and expelled by society. "The higher classes in Russia have no idea how deeply our merchants, tradespeople, and peasants concern themselves about the 'unfortunates.' Almsgiving is almost continual." In the total human situation of the people these "unfortunates" bear not only their own misfortune but also in a representative way the misfortune of humanity. Therefore the people suffer with them and love them. The punishment which he suffers frees the conscience of the convict from every consciousness of guilt. "He has already endured punishment at its hands, and for that reason almost considers himself purged and even with society. There are points of view in fact from which one is almost brought to justify the criminals."

In the church "they prayed humbly, zealously, abasing themselves and fully conscious of their humble state." They put their
poor penny in the collection as though to say "I, too, am a
man" and felt as they gave it, "in God's eyes we are all equal."
When the priest with the chalice in his hand spoke the words:
" '. . . accept me O Lord even as a thief,' almost all of them bowed
down to the ground with a clanking of chains, apparently applying the words literally to themselves."

This is to say, however, that the prisoner, whatever crime he
has committed according to the law of society, is in his suffering
the just one, the free one, indeed something like a saint or martyr
of the suffering people. No convict considers himself not guilty
but neither does any consider himself guilty merely in an individual way. The prisoners bear humanity's burden of guilt, therefore their suffering has a liberating power. What they have done
is meaningless, what they must do in penal labor is meaningless.
But for themselves and for the people their agonies have a redeeming significance. This inner unity of *imprisonment* and *freedom,*
of *suffering* and *redemption,* is no longer the psychological but
rather the religious dimension in the "house of the dead." This is
certainly intended at the close of Dostoevsky's book. When the
prisoner's time was up and his fetters were hacked off, the convicts said in coarse, gruff voices in which, however, there could be
detected a note of pleasure: "Well, with God's blessing, with God's
blessing!" Dostoevsky closes the book with the words: "Yes, with
God's blessing! Freedom, new life, resurrection from the dead. . . .
What a glorious moment!"

Raskolnikov also acknowledged his crime without a merely individual remorse. He also dreamed of the land of freedom on the
other side and his yearning disquieted him. Yet Dostoevsky speaks
of him quite paradoxically: "But now, in prison, *in freedom,* he
pondered. . . ." Through Sonia's love he experienced "the dawn
of a new future," a totally new birth even in his cell, in fetters.
With this, "life had stepped into the place of theory and something
quite different would work itself out of his mind." He also looked
forward to the end of his imprisonment, but his "resurrection from
the dead" happened already in the house of the dead. It did not

happen only with the departing word—"with God's blessing"—
at his release but already with his "Yes" to the reality of his suffering, for which Sonia's love had prepared the murderer.

Imprisonment and hope, the dream of freedom and homeless-
ness, define the *situation of man*. Dostoevsky illustrates this in the
lives of prisoners. But the prisoners who accept their suffering and
bear it patiently are the only truly free people in the world. The
"unhappy" are the redeemers. The humiliated are the liberators.
These guilty ones are they who are truly without guilt. This is
the revelation of *true humanity* in that situation between imprisonment and hope. It is not their dream which liberates the
unfortunate. Rather through their suffering they contribute to
the liberation of humanity. And when love reaches them, resurrection from the dead occurs already in the midst of the house of
the dead.

With this insight we have come already to the second truth
which I have learned from Dostoevsky. He called it resurrection
(*Auferstehung*) and meant by that the dawn of a new life (*die
Morgenröte eines neuen Lebens*).

The truth comes from the story of Sonia Semenvna, the prostitute, the child of God, and of the student Raskolnikov who is
made into the murderer of an old woman by his Napoleonic visions of omnipotence.[3] Sonia is the most defenseless and grace-filled
of all of Dostoevsky's female figures. She is the child of God who
opens up the kingdom of God, that kingdom of freedom, which is
closed to the great and the wise.

As Raskolnikov looks at her, he sees on her face Lizaveta's childlike terror before he murdered her. Sonia looks at him with the
same fear. "Her terror infected him. The same fear showed itself
in his face. In the same way he stared at her and almost with the
same *childish* smile." Her defenselessness before him transformed
him. As she told him of the frightful misery of her home which
had led her to prostitution, "an inexhaustible sympathy, if one
may express it so, lay in her face." This "inexhaustible sympathy"
enabled her to bear any foreboding fate. She is without self-
concern and without fear. She does not make judgments; she
neither condemns nor justifies. She experiences Raskolnikov's

foreboding destiny as her own. And Raskolnikov finds in this girl's inexhaustible sympathy for him a way out of his theories about life into real life. He comes to know himself through her.

As a result, the confession of the murderer finally takes place in the arms of the inexhaustible sympathy of this defenseless girl. "What have you done—what have you done to yourself?" she said in utter despair. As he disclosed his crime, she jumped up from her knees, "flung herself on his neck, threw her arms around him, and held him tightly." Raskolnikov drew back and looked at her with a mournful smile. "You are a strange girl, Sonia, you kiss me and hug me when I tell you that. . . . You don't know what you are doing." "No," she cried as if in a frenzy, "there is no one in the whole world now so unhappy as you!" Then she broke into hysterical weeping. At that moment "a feeling long unfamiliar to him flooded into his heart. Two tears started into his eyes and hung on his eyelashes."

This story is as peculiar as the story of Jesus' encounter with the woman who was a great sinner. There is absolutely no law, no startled glance at the pernicious crime, no reproach. Immediately and without reflection the "inexhaustible sympathy" responds: "What have you done to yourself—no one in the whole world now is so unhappy as you." This goes deeper than any superficial morality; from behind the hateful crime, the unhappy man comes into view. The love, the embrace, the kiss are meant for him. This is very biblical: punishment is already present in the sin itself, Godforsakenness is already present in Godlessness, and evil itself already embraces the resulting unhappiness. Dostoevsky says: "There are no criminals and no judges, there are only the accused." "You turned away from God and God has smitten you, has given you over to the devil!" says Sonia. Raskolnikov, still dreaming the law's dream of revenge, does not understand. Yet he recognizes the truth of her life. He bends down, throws himself on the floor, and kisses her foot. Sonia draws back from him terrified. "What is wrong with you? What are you doing? Before me?" He stands up: "I did not bow down to you, I bowed down to all suffering humanity." For him also the great suffering of Sonia is more important than her disgrace and sin with which she wanted to save her family but could not. For her, also, everything was "for nothing," and in a double sense. "You have killed and sold yourself for nothing," Raskolnikov tells her quite rightly.

Then he asks her, "So you pray to God a great deal, Sonia?" At first she says nothing and then she whispers "What would I be without God?" "And what does God do for you?" he asks, pressing her further. Sonia is at first not able to answer, and then she whispers quickly, "He does everything for me." This goes beyond every utilitarian reason: there is in it neither advantage nor disadvantage. Sonia loves God "for nothing" because God loves her "for nothing" out of his pure grace: "He does everything for me." This grace which does not judge and does not defend, this inexhaustible sympathy is itself Sonia's secret of God.

We come now to the unforgettable scene in which the New Testament speaks, without exposition and interpretation. Raskolnikov picks up the Bible of the murdered Lizaveta. He demands that Sonia read the story of the resurrection of the already stinking body of the poor Lazarus. Full of shame and reverence she reads him the story, and it dawns upon him that it is her own story. With the words of John's Gospel, "he who believeth in me, though he were dead, yet shall he live, and whosoever liveth and believeth in me shall never die," she confesses her own faith, "Yes, Lord: I believe that thou art the Christ, the Son of God which should come into the world."

As she read, "And he that was dead came forth," she whispers abruptly to Raskolnikov, "That is all about the raising of Lazarus." "The candle-end was flickering out in the battered candlestick, dimly lighting up in the poverty-stricken room the murderer and the harlot who had so strangely been reading together the eternal book."

The harlot stands before the murderer in the place of Christ, as Jesus stood before the stinking corpse of Lazarus. Then she accompanies him, through the ordeal of confessing his guilt and suffering the punishment, all the way to imprisonment in Siberia. And there, what spoke to both of them in that hour of truth is realized: resurrection and life. There in prison he flings himself to her feet; he weeps and throws his arms around her knees. "A light of infinite happiness came into her eyes. She knew and had no doubt that he loved her beyond everything. . . . Those sick pale faces were bright with the dawn of a new future, of a full resurrection into a new life."

Dostoevsky closes the story of Raskolnikov with the words: "But that is the beginning of a new story—the story of the gradual renewal of a man, the story of his gradual regeneration, of his passing from one world into another, of his initiation into a new unknown life." He did not write the second story, the story of the resurrected Raskolnikov. One cannot actually *write* it: one can only live it. In this world, resurrection happens where inexhaustible sympathy reaches the unhappy one and he accepts his suffering. For at that moment the proud and unhappy superman, who sees his neighbor only as "a louse" to be crushed, becomes a sinner who recognizes his misery. This is the true human being.

In the sympathy of the humiliated Sonia he encounters the "beauty which redeems the world." For the old Raskolnikov one idea was as good as another. Why should his ideas be any more stupid than the other theories which buzz through the world? But in prison the new Raskolnikov was born to "real life" through the love of Sonia. The superman becomes a man, the theory of power gives way to the true life of love. In the "house of the dead" he understands Sonia's God: "He does everything for me." He becomes a man with a "new perspective on life." He is with the sinners and tax collectors, with whom Jesus is present; he is with the unhappy, who redeem the world; he is with the suffering ones, who are able to love inexhaustibly. Dostoevsky's "resurrection of the dead" does not storm heaven with Prometheus, but descends into the midst of the dead among whom alone resurrection can happen. It comes to the sinners among whom alone forgiveness is near; it comes to the miserable among whom there is grace; it comes into the shadows of the Godforsaken crucified one, shadows which, in a paradoxical way, are already the dawn of the new future of the resurrection.

Dostoevsky's "Christianity was a Christianity of tax collectors and criminals," says Fyodor Stepun. His conception of resurrection led him to humiliation and communion with the "unhappy." "Love men in their sins," says the Elder Zossima in *The Brothers Karamazov*, "love one another and have no fear of the sins of men: the love for sins is already divine love." Then comes the supremely paradoxical sentence, which was later omitted from the novel, "Love sin." What is "love"? "Loving humility is marvelously strong, the strongest of all things and there is nothing else like it," says the Elder. It is the power of the people which is never grasped by their rulers and controllers.

Dostoevsky's God might be indeed none other than the crucified Christ, the Godforsaken Son of God. The defenseless, humiliated Christ who expressed inexhaustible sympathy, the homeless, powerless brother of the "unhappy" was the "Lord God" of Russian folk piety. The suffering people understood him because they felt they were understood by him. He was not the heavenly Pantocrator, represented by the czar and the great church, but the poor Christ, represented by the "idiot," by the "ridiculous man," by the grace-filled harlot, Sonia. From a dogmatic perspective this view of Christ is perhaps an inheritance of monophysitic theology and kenotic theology. But certainly in Dostoevsky's case it embodied the messianic faith that resurrection comes near to the world in the cross just as redemption comes near in suffering, exaltation in humiliation, and glorification in inexhaustible sympathy.

For him, resurrection and new life begin with taking up one's cross, whatever personal humiliation and deprivation might be involved in it. This truth of the human God and the human person is being lost today where a society or even a revolution establishes itself and defends its new order through law and morality, through hatred for the state's enemies and through prisons. Life becomes inhuman; it becomes superficial. Work and consumption have the effect of repressing suffering, one's own as well as the other's. And when suffering is repressed, so is love. Finally, with the loss of love, comes the demise of interest in life. One walks over dead bodies and one becomes a living corpse. The world is changed into a "house of the dead," where dead relationships turn life into numbness and torpidity. The way to resurrection in such a world of dead, inhuman mechanism comes only through suffering, the acceptance of boundless suffering, and transfiguration brought about by the grace of love and the hope of the unhappy.

With this I come to my last point, to the truth of *messianism* in Dostoevsky. It is often passed over in painful silence or referred to with many reservations by Western European interpreters of his work. Thurneysen says, "Defending him here would mean misunderstanding him."[4] Others view him as a fanatic Panslavist. Guardini speaks of the Asiatic immoderate Russian soul as opposed to the moderate and balanced Roman Catholic mentality.

Dostoevsky was indeed convinced of the holy mission of Russia, of his people, and of his church. But is this Russian nationalism? According to Dostoevsky, every Russian yearns "for a unity of all men." "Perhaps being a Russian, becoming totally a Russian means nothing other than becoming a brother with all other men, unfolding oneself into the whole of humanity." The Russian people are not called to conflict but "to proclaim the ultimate word of universal harmony, to realize the ultimate reconciliation of all peoples and tribes in the spirit of the gospel." For Dostoevsky, Russia's world mission did not spring from her positive values, her achievements, but from her patient endurance of the world, from her suffering and the capacity of her people for inexhaustible sympathy, from Orthodoxy's religious idea of *sobernost*—community based on the principle of conciliation. For this reason he was anti-Western; for this reason he also rejected the technocratic revolution. In the suffering of the Russian people, in the suffering of the "unhappy" and in inexhaustible compassion he saw the Christ-gestalt of the Russian people. He combined his love for the people with the idea of self-sacrifice for the redemption of humanity. This is more than Panslavism and more than Russian patriotism. It is rather that *resurrection of the human being* which Karl Marx called the "human emancipation of man."

In this way Dostoevsky was actually a prophet of the "Russian peoples' revolution" of 1917, as the first Soviet commissar of education, Lunacharsky, still called him in 1925:

Russia seemed to him a self-willed and boundless soul, an ocean of elusive contradictions. But precisely this . . . Russia, he believed, would advance toward great and heroic action and in the midst of tribulations strive for the achievement of great goals in the gleaming future of mankind. . . . Russia exercises in fact the role of the leader of the whole world, of the proletariat in the West and the colonial slaves in the East. If Dostoevsky were now to rise from the dead, he would be able poetically to convince us all of the full necessity of our heroic

actions and of the sacredness of the cross (!) which we are bearing on
our shoulders. He would teach us to find satisfaction in this action,
pleasure in these sufferings and, with eyes which simultaneously
divulge horror and enthusiasm, to follow the clamorous torrent of
revolution. . . . Russia is taking the lead in these powerful ways, and
behind Russia, as if giving blessing in these ways, stand the figures of
her great prophets, among them perhaps the most alluring and beautiful figure—Fyodor Dostoevsky.[5]

But was Dostoevsky, and with him the messianic suffering of
the Russian people, the prophet and the mainstay of Stalinist
bureaucracy—trust is good, control is better (Stalin)—of state
atheism, and of a conformist church which Solzhenitsyn has recently attacked? Fyodor Stepun maintained:

Only one thing is unambiguously clear, that Dostoevsky would have
struggled unconditionally and without compromise against Leninist
socialism as theory and practice. He unquestionably would have agreed
with the anathema which the Patriarch Tichon pronounced at the beginning of 1918 against the government of the Bolshevik party. In the
heroic and self-sacrificing struggle of the persecuted church against the
anti-Christ government Dostoevsky undoubtedly would have played a
leading role as a standardbearer and defender of what was essential.
. . . What the Russian people's revolution was really yearning for cannot be further examined here. One thing only is certain, that its stormy
compusion craved things of much greater dimensions than the realization of the rationalist-materialist doctrine of Karl Marx and Friedrich
Engels.[6]

Who is right? The Commissar Lunacharsky or the emigrant
Stepun? Without a doubt the Bolshevik proletarian myth acquired
to no small degree its dynamic buoyancy and its roots in the people
from the charismatic suffering of Russian messianism. This understanding of the "heroic deed and the holiness of the cross" among
the masses, of which Lunacharsky spoke, was a great resource for the
proletarian myth. But has the messianism of the suffering people
found revolutionary fulfillment in the form of the new Russia
represented by Stalin and Krushchev? Every historical fulfillment
of a hope brings with it a disappointment. Thus the hopes of the
people are scaled down by these rulers from the initial horizons
to satisfaction with the new socialist achievements. And even at

best there arises that "melancholy of fulfillment" (Ernst Bloch) which produces new despair.

Dostoevsky as "prophet of the revolution," as Merezhkovsky called him in a book title, is a dangerous memory, not only for Westerners and the West but also for the custodians of the revolution in the Soviet Union.

Dostoevsky was no a radical of the left, as Lunacharsky wanted to make him out, and certainly not a radical of the right, as Fyodor Stepun wanted to fashion him. According to his understanding, "revolution means nothing other than an incessant mission forward, a commitment to remain on the way, on the way of a protest for the cause of the betrayed, misused, exploited, and controlled men and women in East and West."[7] On this "revolution of man," on this "resurrection of man" from his "houses of death" in West and East, on the wholeness of mankind and an inexhaustible sympathy with the "unhappy," Dostoevsky is still waiting. One can forget him in the West because he is not sufficiently positive or moral. One can refuse to print him because the remembrance of him is dangerous for the establishment, as is the case from time to time in the East. But the people and the unhappy ones keep bearing his hope on.

It is thus appropriate to close with a poem by Yevtushenko which has made alive again something of the spirit of Dostoevsky, the spirit of the prisoners and their hope, of their freedom in imprisonment and of the "resurrection of the dead":

> Give us, God:
> no house,
> and no success,
> nor the dull pleasantness of everyday.
> Give us, God:
> the grace, wherever we meet,
> to stand on the bridge.
> On the bridge,
> eternally cutting into the heavens,
> on the bridge,
> sanctified for all time,
> on the bridge,
> an arch over the times,
> over everything,
> lies and vanity. . . .[8]

NOTES TO CHAPTER SEVEN

1. The quotations are from Fyodor Dostoevsky, *The House of the Dead,* trans. Constance Garnett (New York: Dell, 1959). (Translation is slightly altered in places.)
2. Cf. M. Doerne, *Gott und Mensche in Dostojewskijs Werk,* 2d ed. (Göttingen: Vandenhoeck & Ruprecht, 1962), p. 24.
3. The quotations are from Fyodor Dostoevsky, *Crime and Punishment,* trans. Constance Garnett (New York: Bantam Books, 1958).
4. Eduard Thurneysen, *Dostojewskij,* 3d ed. (Zürich: Gotthelf-Verlag, 1963), p. 61.
5. Emmanuel Sarkisyanz, *Russland und der Messianismus des Orients* (Tübingen: J. C. B. Mohr [Paul Siebeck], 1955), p. 132.
6. Fyodor Stepun, *Dostojewskij. Weltshau und Weltanschauung* (Heidelberg: C. Pfeffer, 1950), pp. 71, 77.
7. Johannes Harder, *Proteste. Stimmen russischer Revolutionare aus zwei Jahrhunderten* (Wuppertal: Jugenddienst-Verlag, 1963), p. 15.
8. Ibid., pp. 247–248.

VIII.

Political Theology

Recently the call for a "political theology" has furnished a new bogey for all those who are seeking only peace and quiet in the church and only inner tranquility in faith. We should ask just what political theology today really is and whether Christian theology can become a political theology.

If a preacher uses his pulpit to make political speeches instead of proclaiming the Word of God to faith or if, on the other hand, a politician uses his campaign speeches for making pious, high-flown remarks instead of delivering a clear political program to the people, we all have an uneasy feeling. Politicizing theologians and pietizing politicians are neither fish nor fowl. Dealing with such mixtures certainly cannot be our object.

But what about Christians in the world? They are left standing between the theologians and the politicians, and they hear both sides. They live in the church as well as in politics. Somehow they must bring together their personal faith and their public political interest. This, however, is becoming an increasingly difficult assignment for Christians today. Thus some abandon all interest in politics and retreat with their faith into the private dimension of their innermost piety and childhood training. To them politics seems like a "dirty business." Others abandon all interest in faith and the church because they find there no help for mastering political problems. To them religion seems like an illusion which they cannot abide.

The *Sitz im Leben* of political theology today is the life of Christians in the world. It is the theological reflection of Christians who for the sake of their consciences suffer in the midst of the public misery of society and struggle against this misery.

During the Third Reich, Dietrich Bonhoeffer pointedly reminded the church that "only those who cry out for the Jews may sing Gregorian chants," and he gladly sang Gregorian chants. The memory of what happened at that time has made us increasingly aware that we also have no right to speak of God and with God if we do not do it in the midst of the conflicts of our political world.

I

But what then are we to mean by the Christians' "political theology"?

The historical-critical sciences of the Enlightenment created in modern man a consciousness of the relativity of the Christian tradition which for many centuries had been considered unquestionable and absolute. These traditions are no longer the self-evident receptacles in which we live. Critical faith has achieved a reflective and free relationship with its basic traditions. But today the church, theology, and faith must engage in a social, political, and psychological criticism of the Enlightenment in order to achieve a new state of consciousness. The destiny of man has become more and more a political destiny, but politics has not yet become truly human. Consequently modern criticism asks about the practical, political, and psychic effects of the churches, of theologies, and of ways of believing.

Responsible theology must therefore engage in institutional criticism as it reflects on the "place" of the churches "in the life" of modern society and in ideological criticism as it reflects on itself. It can no longer self-forgetfully screen out its own social and political reality as the old metaphysical and personalistic theologies did. So in public, responsible theology itself stands consciously between the Christian, eschatological message of freedom and the socio-political reality. Thus through an interrogation of institutions, words, and symbols, it must ascertain whether a religious opium is being mediated to the people or a real ferment of freedom; whether faith or superstition is being spread; whether the crucified one is made present or the idols of the nation are served.

Political theology is therefore not simply political ethics but reaches further by asking about the political consciousness of theology itself. It does not want to make political questions the central theme of theology or to give political systems and movements religious support. Rather, political theology designates the field, the milieu, the environment, and the medium in which Christian theology should be articulated today.

Political theology is therefore a hermeneutical category. There is a point of departure for this hermeneutical category in former theological research, namely, in the form-historical criticism of the biblical texts. Every literary genre represents simultaneously a sociological fact. This exegetical perception prevents the simple distinction between intellectual and political history. Should not the form-historical method be capable of being directed toward present life and the contemporary expressions of life? A pure hermeneutic of understanding intellectual history of course makes us conscious of the historicity of the individual, but it represses into the unconscious the historicity of the social and political conditions in which individuals live.

It is therefore only consistent to move from the existentialist and personalistic interpretations of traditional texts to a political hermeneutic of these traditions and from a hermeneutic of pure understanding to an exegesis of traditional religious representations in practical intent. As Marcuse has written, "The memory of the past can allow dangerous insights to arise and the established society seems to be afraid of the subversive content of memories." Political theology would like to try to interpret the dangerous memory of the messianic message of Christ within the conditions of contemporary society in order to free man practically from the coercions of this society and to prepare the way for the eschatological freedom of the new man.

II

If Christian theology becomes in this sense a political theology, it encounters in society contradictions and adversaries which often bear the same name, that is, the civil religion of a society and its ideological formulation in political theology. Thus at this point we need an historical excursus in order to make clear what was meant and what is meant by political theology.

Political religions are not the discovery of Christianity. They are the essence of ancient pagan religions in which there are no states without gods and no divinities without states. Since its origin in the Christ who was crucified for political reasons, the Christian

faith has always had to struggle against the political religions of
the nations.

The expression *political theology* originated with the philosophy
of the Stoa. Panaetius distinguished three classes of divinity: the
personified powers of nature, the gods of the state religion, and those
of myth (*genus physikon, politikon,* and *mythikon*). With this
scheme he established the *tripartita theologia,* which was imple-
mented in the rationalistic theology of Rome. Plato had already
criticized the mythic theology of the poets under the political
aspects of "city founders" (*Republic* II, 379a). In *De civitate Dei,*
Augustine argued against this political theology of Rome (VI, 12).
The divine images of the poets are mythic, and mythical theology
is best suited for the cultic-public theater. The theological concepts of the philosophers are substantial or metaphysical. Natural
theology belongs to the philosophical school. The names and rites
of the state gods are political.

The Roman Stoic, Varro, considered political theology to be
the highest, for in a commonwealth the citizens and priests must
know which gods have to be recognized on account of the state
and through which holy acts they must be revered. According to
the classical social theory, it is the *finis principalis* of society to
render the proper honor to the gods, for they bless the welfare of
the land. In the late Hellenistic period the *polis,* once an organiza-
tional principle for religious reverence, could itself become an
object of religious reverence. The cities were deified (*Dea Roma*).
What "political religion" meant in antiquity is made beautifully
clear in an ode by Horace:

You will undeservedly suffer for the sins of the fathers, O Rome,
until you restore the temple, rebuild the fallen houses of the gods, and
clean the images soiled by smoke and grime.

It is only because you consider yourself subject to the gods that you
rule the world. This is the foundation of everything. Let it remain
your goal. Because it scorned them, the gods struck grieving Rome with
many blows. (III, 6)

In his investigation, *The Reproach of Atheism in the First Three
Centuries (Der Vorwurf des Atheismus in den ersten drei Jahrhunderten,* 1905), Adolf von Harnack demonstrated that this po-

litical religion was compelling only in terms of its public practice. The merely theoretical or purely private disavowal of the state gods, however, was not yet considered to be *crimen laesae religionis* but only the neglect of the public duties of religion. Only in the framework of this religious *raison* of state was the accusation of atheism lodged against Christians. Justin Martyr, in view of the *Dei populi Romani,* openly referred to himself as an "atheist." But ever since the legislation of the Christian emperors Theodosius and Justinian, the relations have been reversed; the Christian religion has been looked upon as a state religion—*religio licita,* while the Jewish religion has been viewed as sacrilege and non-Christian religions as a species of atheism.

Since Constantine and the process of Christianization of Europe, Christianity often has taken over the role of the nations' political religions wherever it has encountered them. Of course, it has "Christianized" the existing state religions, but at the same time it has been "politicized" in the sense of the current *raison* of state. Therefore, we cannot really speak of the Christian churches in European societies as being nonpolitical. Precisely because today they often consider themselves nonpolitical and want always to remain socially in the neutral middle, they fulfill needs in the fashion of a political religion; that is, they provide for the symbolic integration of society and its homogenization and self-confirmation.

Therefore, we must ask whether the social *topos* of political religion is present also in modern societies which call themselves "pluralistic," "secularized," and "emancipated." And if it is, we should ask who fills out and formulates this *topos* today. I think that present-day sociology and psychology of religion show that the *topos* "political religion" has in no way vanished from modern societies. Political religion is found wherever a society integrates itself with the help of symbols and a nation represents its origins, its struggles for existence, its destiny, and, therefore, its self-consciousness in mythicized stories. One can find it in national memorials and holidays, in cemeteries and symbols of dignity, in presidential addresses and school books. Political religion is found in confessional form, in universal-Christian form, in biblical-religious form, in Shintoist, Islamic, and Buddhist form, and not least of all in the form of atheistic state ideologies. A comparison between the

symbols and myths of the Soviet Union—Lenin mausoleum and
the October Revolution—and the symbols and myths of the
United States can make this clear.

III

As is well known, however, early Christianity, as the following
of him who was crucified, was considered by pagan philosophers
(Celsus), as well as the Roman Senate, to be godless. For this reason it was viewed as an enemy of the state and was persecuted. So
much the more did Christian apologists make it their business to
expound the Christian faith as the true religion capable of preserving the state and Christian theology as the higher political
theology. In his magnificent treatise, *Monotheism as Political
Problem (Monotheismus als politisches Problem*, 1935), Erik Peterson sketched the political history of theological ideas in early
church dogmatics. Where do we find the connections and the
unbridgeable differences between political metaphysics and Christian faith in God?

Quite early Christian philosophers united biblical monotheism
with philosophical monotheism. A scrutiny of metaphysical monotheism, however, reveals that it was a monarchism. If there is only
one God, there is also only one ruler on earth. The Universal itself
has a hierarchical-monarchical structure: one God—one *logos*—
one cosmos. Divinity is the symbol and integration point for the
unity of reality as a whole. The monotheism of this "natural
theology" corresponds to the imperialism of the one emperor in
the related "political theology."

This convertibility of metaphysical into political and political
into metaphysical concepts is already recognizable in Aristotle
himself. He concludes his theologic in the twelfth book of his
metaphysics with the sentence: "The creatures refuse to be governed badly. It is not good to have many rulers. Let there be one
Lord." This is a quotation which originates as a saying of
Agamemnon in *The Iliad* where it was intended politically.

This correspondence between world view and the foundation of
the state can be traced into modern times. The Christian apologists
appropriated this convertibility of concepts in order to turn the
early Christian denial of the Roman emperor cult into a Christian

foundation of the Roman Empire of peace. The people of the one God coming together in the one church from many peoples and tongues is superior to the polytheism of the many religions. The conception of unity in God and the conception of unity in the church evoke, so to speak, the corresponding political conception of unity. "To the one king on earth there corresponds the one God, the one King in heaven, and the one kingly *nomos* and *logos*" (Peterson).

Thus the Christian apologists united Christ's kingdom of peace with the idea of *Pax Romana*. For as Eusebius explained, when the Savior appeared on earth, and simultaneously with his arrival Augustus as the first among the Romans became lord over the nations, the rule of many on earth was dissolved, and peace embraced the whole world. Christianity became the inner religion of the external Roman empire of peace. Out of this emerged the first Christian political theology of Christianity: one God—one Savior —one emperor—one church—one kingdom.

Erik Peterson has demonstrated that this political-religious monotheism was destroyed by the inner power of the Christian faith itself. This took place at two basic points: the trinitarian doctrine of God and the eschatological concept of peace. The development of the doctrine of the Trinity caused a disintegration of political metaphysics, for the mystery of the three-in-oneness exists solely in God himself and not as a political image in the creature. Christian theology intends the doctrine of the Trinity as a paraphrase of the unity of God the Father with the crucified Christ in the Holy Spirit. If the revelation of God in the crucified one—and not in mere speculation—is the real beginning point for the doctrine of the Trinity, then the Christian doctrine of God can no longer be used as religious background material for the ruling authorities, principalities, and powers.

This criticism of political metaphysics remains even today, I think, the political inference of the doctrine of the Trinity. Christianity is not a "monotheistic kind of belief," as Schleiermacher insisted, and not "radical monotheism," as H. Richard Niebuhr said, but trinitarian faith. The liberal sacrifice of the doctrine of the Trinity is the sign for the unconscious dissolution of Christian faith in the political religion of a "Christian world."

On the other hand, the equation of *Pax Christi* with *Pax Romana* could never really succeed because of the infinite quality of Christian hope. The peace of God is secured and maintained not by any Caesar or ideology of power, but alone by the crucified one. Therefore, it is a peace which is higher than all reason—even political reason. The peace of God is furthermore a universal peace and therefore cannot be limited to the boundaries of the *Pax Romana* or of a "Christian world." Should not this hope, which is constantly becoming greater, also bring present-day Christians into a critical distance between the ideas of *Pax Americana* and *Pax Sovietica* and technocratic and revolutionary conceptions of peace?

For Erik Peterson, the development of the doctrine of the triune God and of the eschatological concept of peace has forced Christian theology into a fundamental break with every political theology. For him, there is no longer any political theology in Christianity. But it seems to me that the political problems of Christian theology only begin at this point.

IV

These problems lie concretely in the relationship of Christian faith to the political religion of a particular country. We can exemplify them by turning to the dissimilar assessments of the phenomena of American civil religion by two sociologists of religion: Robert Bellah and Peter Berger.

In his well-known article, "Civil Religion in America" (*Daedalus*, 1967), Robert Bellah uses the inaugural speeches of American presidents to point out that in the country which has been noted for a strict separation of church and state, there is a peculiar, new political religion. It has its own distinctive character, its own existence, and its own independent development. In its appeal to the pilgrim fathers it is messianic: exodus and chosen people. In its appeal to the Old Testament prophets it is socio-critical and "revolutionary," as John F. Kennedy emphasized. In its veneration of Abraham Lincoln it finds its martyrdom: "The dead have died that the nation might live."

More recently this political religion discovered a typical focus of enmity—"communism." But it is neither Protestant nor Catholic nor Jewish. It is capable of mobilizing the people for new efforts and struggles such as were embodied in Roosevelt's "New Deal," Kennedy's "New Frontier," and the Civil Rights Movement. It can lead to the national "arrogance of power" (Fulbright) in the radicalism of the right or the religion of the hard-hats as well as to the spreading of the American way of life as a special blessing to the world. Robert Bellah's criticism of this civil religion of his country works only with the distinction between particularism and universalism: "As Americans we have been well favored in the world, but it is as men that we will be judged."

With respect to its best intentions, "a world civil religion" could be viewed as the fulfillment and not the destruction of the "American dream." "Indeed such an outcome has been the eschatological hope of American civil religion from the beginning." Should it also become the Christian-ecumenical dream that out of the Christian national religion there should arise a world civil religion as the religion of humanity for a unified mankind? Many ecumenical expressions take this direction.

As early as 1961 in *The Noise of Solemn Assemblies: Christian Commitment and the Religious Establishment in America,* however, Peter Berger had already described this civil religion in the United States in a quite similar way, but had viewed the task of Christians as one of "disestablishment." "The God of Moses, who refused to give his name for magical uses, is the same God who comes to us in Jesus Christ." "It would perhaps be significant for our pious hygienists of the soul to remember that Jesus of Nazareth was crucified." "We think in our situation the theological task is to elaborate the eschatological character of the Christian faith against the this-worldliness of American religiosity, to set the justification by faith against our pervasive legalism, to explain the meaning of the cross in a culture which glorifies success and happiness." Berger does not only consider this a Christian task, for the denial of the civil white religion constitutes an important element in what one could call "the other America," in that America which is denounced in the "community of the respectable."

We have before us two clear judgments about American civil religion. They prompt us to ask the question: Is the universalization of the Christianized civil religions of Europe and America in the form of a civil religion of the world a goal for which we should be striving? Or, can the Christian hope make its universalism concrete only when, for the sake of the crucified one, it enters into a critical iconoclasm against the existing civil religions and simultaneously enters into solidarity with those who are oppressed by the civil religion of a society and are forcibly excluded? Where is the Christian eschatology of which Bellah and Berger are speaking? Is it in the universalism of a civil religion bound up with a coming world society or in the dialectic of the cross?

V

If we can designate something which is beyond all doubt irreplaceably Christian, it is the relation of all theological statements, even eschatological statements of hope, to the cross of Christ. The cross is the point at which Christian faith distinguishes itself from other religions and ideologies, from unfaith and superstition. It is worthy of note that the cross of Christ is also the one truly political point in the story of Jesus. It should therefore become the beginning point and the criterion for a Christian political theology.

Jesus was condemned according to the law of Israel as a blasphemer. Paul and the Reformers again and again made a theological interpretation of the fact that Jesus died at the hands of the law and that consequently the law with its demands comes to an end at the hands of the resurrected one. If Jesus, the one condemned according to the law, is the Christ of God, then man is made righteous no longer by the works of the law, but through faith. For all those who are godless and unrighteous, the "Word of the cross," the gospel, becomes the power of liberation from the curse of the law.

Jesus was not killed by stoning, the punishment for blasphemy, a punishment which the Jews of his time were authorized to carry out, as is obvious in the case of Stephen. Jesus was crucified by the Romans. Crucifixion was a political punishment for political agitators against the *Pax Romana* and was used exclusively by the Roman authorities. Certainly Jesus was no Zealot freedom-fighter against the Roman occupation force. Thus, the immediate legal ground for his execution by Pilate was perhaps feeble.

But is there not implicit in his eschatological message of freedom for sinners and of the coming kingdom for the poor a much greater attack against the religiously deified state? Did he not cause with this message an "agitation" in the political situation of Rome which was much more radical than the one caused by the Jewish Zealots? In this sense, his crucifixion was quite consistently political, not an accident or an error. The Christian martyrs who were sent into the arena still knew that quite well. They also knew, as the book of Revelation notes, what Rome could be as a power of repression. Should not Christian theology therefore interpret the political fact of the crucifixion theologically in order to unroll again the public trial *"aut Christus—aut Caesar"*?

From Hegel's observations in the *Philosophy of Religion* about the external polemical side of Jesus' death, we can gather the following basic references: If the one profaned with crucifixion by the authority of the state is the Christ of God, then what is lowest in the political imagination is changed into what is highest. What the state had considered the deepest humiliation, namely, the cross, bears the highest dignity. When the cross is raised as a standard, whose positive content is the kingdom of God, then the life of the state is deprived of its inner disposition, that is, religion. For those who recognize the Christ of God in the crucified one, the glory of God no longer shines on the crowns of the mighty but alone on the face on the tortured Son of man. If this crucified one becomes divine authority for the believers, the political-religious faith in authority ceases to hold sway over them. For them, the political forces are deprived of direct religious justification from above.

From these few observations it is clear first of all that the Christian faith, for the sake of the crucified one, cannot accommodate itself to the political religions of the societies in which it lives. Rather, if it wants to maintain its identity as Christian faith, it must become the power of liberation from them. Adolf Schlatter said in this regard, "The vocation and work of Jesus consists in his destroying our idols, and the weapons with which he nullifies our false gods is his cross." Because there are few spheres of life more beset by idolatry and alienation than politics, we must devote our attention to the means of accomplishing liberation in it.

We can begin our consideration of the problem with two theses:

(1) The Old Testament prohibition of images says: "You shall not make yourself a graven image or any likeness of anything. You shall not bow down to them or serve them." It forbids not only religious idolatry but also political idolatry. What was criticized biblically as idolatry emerges again in modern times as criticism of man's alienation and tutelage.

(2) The Christian faith in the crucified one is a radical realization of the Old Testament prohibition of images, specifically (a) in mythical theology by way of demythologization, and (b) in political theology by way of the fundamental democratization of the conditions of rule.

According to the Second Commandment, the worship of gods, superstition, idolatry, fetishism, personality cults, etc., arise out of the fact that men make for themselves a visible image of the invisible God and worship a work of their own hands in order to gain self-confirmation and self-security from it. If idolatry was for the Old Testament the gravest of all sins, Paul took up the criticism (Rom. 1:18ff.) and even turned it around in the criticism of "works righteousness." It is not only that man "makes" himself images of gods, but also that he idolizes, under the constraint of self-justification, everything he "makes" or "does," his good deeds and his great achievements. This works righteousness is "idolatry" because it makes men slaves of their own works by forcing the creators to bow down before their own creations. In the *Larger Catechism*, Luther also summed up the piety of images and works righteousness as the same and pointed to idolatry of the heart as the origin of all sins. "Whatever you set your heart on and depend on, that is really your god."

From a psychological point of view, the unfathomable anxiety of man causes him to create for himself symbols, idols, and values which then become identical with his self. Every attack against his idols threfore wounds his "highest values," and he reacts to this with deadly aggression. As long as his self depends on such idols and idolized realities, man is not free to accept the different kind of life of another along with his own life. He only accepts men who are like him. He only accepts men who value the same things and abhor the same things as he does because these men confirm him.

Strangers put him in question and make him uncertain. Hence the attitude: "Love our country or leave it." This is the basis for xenophobia, anti-Semitism, and racial hatred. The liberation of man from the anxiety and the coercive force of such idols is therefore the presupposition for humanity and peace on earth.

It is a striking fact that since the beginning of modern times the liberation from idolatry has been transferred from Christian theology to the critical sciences. The movements of the Enlightenment can be appropriately represented as the consequent history of the prohibition of images.

Francis Bacon criticized the prejudgments of history as *idola*, as idols which possess the human spirit in such a way that the empirical truth cannot be impartially perceived. The history of the criticism of ideology had its beginning here. Immanuel Kant criticized the dogmatism of reason through the critical reflection of reason on its possibilities and limits and with that reason accepted the absolute boundaries of its concepts. Ludwig Feuerbach's criticism of religion was an explanation of the religious projections of the heart. In terms of criticism this can be quite felicitously understood as negative theology: You shall not make any image or likeness. Sigmund Freud's psychoanalytic explanation of psychic complexes has essentially the same intentions. Karl Marx began consistently with the criticism of religion in order to transfer it to the political and economic alienation of man.

This means in terms of the criticism of religion that "the off-springs of their head have grown up above their head." In terms of the capitalistic society, it means "the creators have bowed down before their creatures." In Marx's later criticism of the "fetish character" of commodities in the capitalistic society of exchange, his earlier beginning point in terms of the criticism of religion emerges again. I think that Christian theology can feel inimical toward these movements of Enlightenment criticism of superstition only to its own detriment and dispense with them only to its own impoverishment.

But how does idolatry and alienation appear in politics? Hobbes already interpreted the prohibition of images politically: "That they should not make any image to represent them, that is to say, they were not to choose to themselves, neither in heaven nor in earth any representative of their own fancying" (*Leviathan,* 42). These observations lead us to the problem of political representation.

A political representation is always necessary if a people wants to become capable of acting in the medium of history. The citizens identify themselves with their representatives and their decisions. They give up the rights of self-determination to their representatives and authorize them to act in their name. However, this necessary representation and substitutions are never without a degree of alienation. "In representative institutions there is always the subordination under a visible image; and that is idolatry" (Norman O. Brown). Political idolatry and political alienation arise when—as Marx made clear—the representatives grow up over the head of those whom they are supposed to represent and when the people bow down before their own government. The consequences then show up in the people's spreading apathy. One no longer identifies himself with the politics of his country's government or his student representatives. Because their representatives elude their control, the citizens fall back into a passivity which simply abets the further misuse of power. These are symptoms of political idolatry; out of representation there develops rule, out of unburdening there develops alienation, out of a functional authority there develops a status authority.

Enlightenment republicanism saw quite clearly this connection between idolatry and political tutelage. "Democracy has no monuments. It strikes no medallions. It does not bear the head of a man on its coins. Its true essence is iconoclasm," said John Quincy Adams, the sixth President of the United States. But if the essence of democracy is political iconoclasm, the interminable process of the permanent democratization of public life is a political fulfillment of the Second Commandment. It serves the freedom of God because it serves the freedom of his image in every man.

The Christian faith calls the crucified one "the image of the invisible God." If it wants to be consistent in its practice, it will therefore forsake and destroy all earthly images and representations of the divine in politics. With the freedom which is opened up to it in the cross it will enter into a permanent iconoclasm against political personality cults and national religions and against money and commodity fetishism. It seems to me that Christians should lead the way in the desacralization and democratization of political rule. Indeed this stands in the compass of their authentic traditions.

It follows for the Christian churches that they must fulfill further their old task of employing the Word of the cross to destroy religious idolatry and personal fetishism and to spread the freedom of faith into the very hovels of the obscure. Its new task then will lie in struggling against not only religious superstition but also political idolatry, not only religious alienation of man but also his political, social, and racial alienation in order to serve the liberation of man to his likeness to God in all areas where he suffers from inhumanity. In this sense, I think, it would also be the task of the churches today to develop "social critical freedom" in institutions. I say "also" because man is basically enslaved by anxiety, and liberation from anxiety happens in the first place through faith—not through social improvements.

VI

A political theology of the cross has deeper dimensions. It would be shortsighted to fix our attention only on the relationship between church and state in order to make out of the church-state marriage a cooperative relationship of freer, more reciprocal criticism. According to the biblical traditions, the church in a state has to do essentially also with those for whom there is virtually no "state at all." Despite the covenant and the nation, there runs through the Old Testament the realization: "You are a God of the wretched, the refuge of the oppressed, the sustainer of the meek, the defense of the forsaken, the savior of the despairing." According to the Magnificat (Lk. 1:46–54), this God flings the mighty from their throne and exalts the lowly.

Jesus' proclamation and deeds were valid for all men precisely because he took sides with the meek, the poor, and the victims of discrimination. Jesus grasped human society, so to speak, at the lowest extreme, where he found the miserable and the disdained. Paul said the gospel is for all men, but he went one-sidedly to the Gentiles in order to save the Jews.

If we comprehend this partisanship of God and of the gospel, we will also discover again the subversive and revolutionary character of the Bible which has been concealed too long under dreams of humanity. The message of the cross is a glad message for the poor. For the rich and the self-righteous, it is quite distressing. The future of God begins in this world, as the Beatitudes show, with the poor, the mourning, the persecuted, and the pure. Christian hope does not surmount the cutting edge of human progress and development. Instead, it seeks out those with whom the crucified one has entered into solidarity and those for whom he has become a brother. These men with whom Christian hope joins itself are the "others." They are men who are forced into nothingness by a self-confirming society which has forced itself into inner homogeneity. According to the inner dialectic of Christian hope, ultimately the rich do not save the poor, but, on the contrary, the poor may save the rich.

How does this happen? I do not mean only where, according to Luke 16, the rich man calls out to Lazarus in the bosom of Abraham, but here on earth. Only the poor really know the oppression of wealth's exclusiveness. Only the hated know the misery which hate causes. The rich, the oppressor, the hater are always a bit oblivious to the misery they cause, even if they are well-intentioned. Therefore, the oppressed hold the key for the liberation of humanity from oppression. If they are filled with Christian hope, then it will not be their intention to become masters where they were once slaves or oppressors where they were once the oppressed, but they are empowered by this hope so far as possible to rid this world utterly of the master-slave relationship and the mechanism of oppression. For Albert Camus, the humane principle of revolt is not the reversal of the master-slave relationship but its elimination. Only then can man associate with man in a human way.

What does this mean for the Christian community? According to an old sentence, the true church is where Christ is: *ubi Christus, ibi Ecclesia*. But where is Christ present? We find in the New Testament two promises of Christ's presence:

(1) Whoever hears you, hears me. Word, sacrament, and the community of the faithful make Christ present.

(2) What you have done to one of the least of these my brothers, you have done to me.

I think that these words from Matthew 25 belong not only in social ethics but primarily in ecclesiology. According to them, there is a double brotherhood of Christ: the one is the manifest brotherhood of the believers; the other is the latent brotherhood of the poor. Thus the Christian community is in the full truth of Christ so long as it realizes this double brotherhood of Christ and is constituted by believers and the poor. It becomes the false church when in its own life it gives validity to the Aristotelian social principle which asserts, by virtue of *philia politike*, "birds of a feather flock together" and, therefore, "one crow does not pick out the eye of another." As civil religion, the church is always subjugated to this principle of homogeneity. It becomes the true church and the sacrament of hope in the new humanity as a community of "others" by virtue of *agape*, that is, the recognition of the other.

Then we find in it, as the Corinthian congregation proclaimed: "Jews" and their opposite "Gentiles," "Greeks" and their opposite "barbarians," "masters" and their opposite "slaves," "whites" and their opposite "blacks." Race, class, status, and national churches smack of heresy in their structures. But when the Christian churches, for the sake of the brotherhood of Christ, join themselves with those who in a particular society are concretely the "others," these churches also concretely dissolve their alliances with those who took the prerogative of declassing the others. They also dissolve their alliances with the prevailing needs for self-confirmation.

If Christian faith is the overcoming of self-righteousness through justification by faith, the church can realize itself only in the political, social, and economic overcoming of self-confirmation through social love. Only then can we surmise something of the beauty of the coming kingdom in the earthly fragments of the church and recognize it as a sacrament of hope in a free, new humanity.

The political theology about which we have inquired does not want to dissolve Christian faith into politics; nor does it want to replace Christianity with humanism. If we would in practice put man in place of the divine, we would theoretically have to put the human essence in place of the divine. If we would change religion into politics, as our "leftist" friends and Marxists demand, politics would have to become our religion. The state or the party would then become the Leviathan, the mortal god on earth. That would mean abolishing once again the desacralization of politics which Christianity has effected. This divinization of politics is a superstition which Christians cannot accept. They are Christians and hold to the crucified one in order to witness to men of a greater freedom.

A Christian "political theology" wants to bring the Christians as Christians, that is, as liberators, to the place where they are being waited upon by the crucified one. In the suffering and condemned ones of this earth, Christ is waiting upon his own and their presence.

The focus of Christian hope is not simply the open future, but the future of the hopeless. The light of the resurrection illuminates the night of the cross and wants to illuminate those who are today consigned to the shadows of the cross. The cross of Christ, the community of the suffering Christ, and the sign of the oppressed creation show us the place of Christian presence.

"The cross alone is our theology," said Luther. Likewise, we contend that the dangerous memory of the cross is our political iconoclasm; the cross is our hope for the politics of liberation. The liberating memory of the crucified Jesus compels Christians to a critical political theology.

IX.

The Ethic of Calvinism

I

"Calvinism" is a very broad and vague term referring to a movement of reforming Christianity which originated in Zurich,
Geneva, and Strasbourg. Throughout its four-hundred-year history
it has assumed various forms in Switzerland, France, Holland,
Hungary, Germany, England, and the United States. The name
originated with the life-work of John Calvin in Geneva, yet (in
contrast to Lutherans) the so-called Calvinists have rarely called
themselves by this name, since they did not want to be followers or
devotees of a man but rather disciples of Jesus Christ. For that
reason there has scarcely emerged a rigidly constructed Calvinistic
orthodoxy. The scriptures and the living experience of the Spirit
stand higher than the confessional writings and the tradition. This
provided the Calvinist movement with a great freedom in the formation of its faith and life.

The historical collective term *Calvinism* thus has nothing to do
with the "ism" of a closed ideology, but rather comprehends,
roughly speaking, those reforming dynamics of the Reformed
churches in Switzerland and Germany, of the Huguenots in
France, of the Congregationalists, Puritans, and Presbyterians in
England and America as well as, more tenuously, the post-Refor-
mation Waldensians in Italy and the Czech Brethren, to name
only a few. Their commonality is to be found less in a unified
dogmatic than in a common will for the consistent realization of
the Reformation in doctrine and life, in church and society. They
are distinguished from the Roman Catholic Church, the Anglican
State Church, and the Lutheran churches more through their
ecclesiastical polity than through theological doctrine. Because its
polity and its practical life style are always related to the concrete
social and political form of a society, the Reformed Church in its

history has been capable of change and has assumed various forms in different cultures.

Reformation faith in the context of the Reformed churches means faith in the permanent reforming and renewing activity of God. "Reformation" no longer means, as in the reform movements of the Middle Ages, the renewal of the church through the work of well-intentioned people, but renewal through the work of God in history. Furthermore, as a movement of the renewal of faith, God's reformation concerns man in his totality, the individual and his relationships in church, society, and state. In view of the close alignment between church and society, it is not adequate simply to reform the church. This was quite often the complaint of Reformed theologians against Lutherans. Upon the heels of the "reformation of doctrine" must follow the *reformation of life,* for, as God's reformation, the renewal is all-encompassing. It is in essence the end-time reformation of the world through that kingdom in which "God will be all in all." The Reformed Church which emerged in Germany in 1563 from the Palatinate Reform (Heidelberg Catechism) considered itself "the second Reformation" or the "completion of the Reformation" of Martin Luther. "Reformation" here was never understood as a unique event to which one could appeal, but rather as a *permanent reformation* and as an open task, always to be experienced and realized anew.

Therefore the churches called themselves *ecclesia reformata et semper reformanda* (the church reformed and constantly in need of reform). This insight into the all-inclusive activity of the reforming Spirit of God can be seen as a peculiar characteristic of "Calvinism." From it stems the determination to place the whole of public life under the command of God, an ethic which extends its critical scrutiny beyond the private morality of individuals into culture and economy, and, finally, the readiness for political resistance to tyranny. The "morality of Calvinism," if it can be so called, is distinguished by a consistent discipleship to Jesus in all areas of life and the comprehensive sanctification of the whole of life for the coming kingdom of God. The following is meant to portray this in the areas of personal life (II), economic ethics (III), and political ethics (IV). The presentation can proceed only with ideal types in order to emphasize important contemporary motifs.

II

For Reformed faith *personal life* stands under the aspects of *calling* and *sanctification*. The faith of the individual no longer consists of participation in a supraindividual, objective, ecclesiastical process into which one is born and which "tends" one from cradle to grave. Living faith stems rather from an *event of calling*. Man is called out of his manifold relationships in religion, society, and state into communion with Christ. In this communion with Christ the old man, who was a slave to the laws of the civil religion, the society surrounding him, and the politics dominating him, dies away. There arises a new person who is liberated to the freedom of Christ. Man is called to participate in the coming glory of God in which the whole groaning creation shall be freed from the humiliation caused by its bondage to decay (Rom. 8:18ff). The call which comes through the Word of the gospel frees man from all godless bonds of this world, but it simultaneously sets him under God's command, which wants to lead him to life and the whole creation to the kingdom of God. Calling and faith liberate man from the "history of death" and place him in the "history of life" (Otto Weber). They do not cause him to flee or scorn the world. Rather they place him in the dawn of God's future which shall break over the whole shrouded world and which has already broken in the appearance of Christ.

From the experience of a personal calling emerges the *task of sanctifying* the whole of worldly life for the kingdom of God. The Reformed faith has thus always understood the command of God and the commandments of the old and the new covenants as guiding principles for the new life lived in faith. To be sure, the command, understood as demand of God, works as a permanent accusation against the sins and neglects of man. It is a mirror in which man recognizes himself in his infinite guilt before God. But it is a mirror which at the same time shows him the crucified Christ who took all of man's guilt upon himself and reconciled him with God. The result is that now man can live, as a creature of God's grace, according to God's commands and through new obedience can conform to God. Reformed theologians have never viewed the command of God merely from the standpoint of sinful, incapacitated man, but rather have understood and interpreted it simultaneously and even more so from the standpoint of the man who is called, justified, and enabled by the Spirit. This has misled many Calvinists and Puritans to a new moralistic legalism. But it has brought to far more Christians joy in the law of God and good conscience in new obedience. It is not the person as sinner with an enduring bad conscience who stands in the foreground but the person who is the covenant partner of the God of grace and the cooperating witness of the coming kingdom. Sanctification means separation, selection, and election to a different life and a particular service. But at the same time sanctification also means transformation of this life, bodily and public obedience, being-for-others.

What were the practical implications of that personal life based on such a calling and lived in the name of sanctification?

Calvin himself was nurtured in French humanist reform. From about 1540 on he distanced himself from his humanist friends. They were all admirers of the Reformation but only in the internal dimension of faith and knowledge. He broke with them because he recognized the integral, uncompromising character of the Reformation as God's reformation, which always involves a re-ordering of all human relationships. He later called these French humanists who were friendly but inconsistent toward the Reformation, "Nicodemites," that is, people who wanted to seek out Jesus at night for conversations with no strings attached, but by day were outwardly obedient to the old order. For Calvin the spreading of the gospel leads inexorably to transformations in society and church order and thus also to collisions and disturbances. He warned against evading these offenses of the gospel simply for the sake of preserving a tranquil and cherished social order. The peace of Christ leads to conflict with this world's organized discord. True peace, peace in righteousness, does not leave the world in its own peace but provokes it.

Was Calvin therefore "revolutionary"? He was certainly no revolutionary in the vein of Thomas Münzer in the peasants' revolt. Throughout the decades, however, the French king justified his bloody persecution of the Protestants by declaring them to be political agitators. Calvin protested against this in open letters.

He rejected the use of violence in the civil war between the Huguenots and the Catholic League in France and encouraged the congregations in their passive resistance and endurance of suffering. The Huguenot Christians nevertheless caused political unrest and were in this sense "revolutionary."

The Reformed congregations in Western and Southern Europe were almost always *minorities*. Their destiny was marked by disadvantage, reprisals, prison, expulsion, emigration, and murder. Even though their faith emphasized their permanent calling, this had nothing to do with an elite consciousness of election. *Election* meant in practice for them *endurance in faith* until the end, resisting all temptations and all coercive measures and demonstrating unflinching perseverance. One must understand the Reformed doctrine of predestination against the background of their experiences of suffering and persecution as well as the amazing resistance of many of these Christians. Otherwise one will not understand it at all. An unforgettable testimony of this is the word *recister* which Marie Durand scratched into the stone wall of the tower of Constance at Aigues-Mortes in Southern France. She was imprisoned in this tower for forty years. When Reformed Christians emphasized sanctification in life, they spoke out of a situation in which they were assailed on all sides. Thus they meant by sanctification that necessary spirit of nonconformism which belongs to Christian existence, the perseverance and steadfastness required to uphold this alien stance, and the persistent overcoming of internal and external oppositions. People have often denounced Calvinist morality as zeal for work, capitalism, and greediness. Their writings do in fact often speak of "work." But by "work" they did not mean "producing," but rather bearing the suffering, pain, and opposition to which life in faith leads.

What speaks to us out of the life history of many Reformed Christians—the Huguenots, Waldensians, Puritans, and Brethren —is the firm certainty of their faith and a stance of resistance against temptation and persecution, which made them unwavering and willing to suffer. The more Christians become a minority today and lose the protection of a "Christian" society, the more they will be able to learn from Calvinist morality to become aliens in their own society and among their own people for the sake of

Christ. In the history of Reformed Christianity the courage to be different becomes visible. Only he who is different *from* others can "be *for* others"; otherwise he is merely together with those who are like him.

III

Since its beginnings in Zurich and Geneva, Reformed Christianity has been alive predominately in the great cities. It was spread in France by merchants and was carried into other countries by emigrants. Thus it formed a certain alliance with the freedom struggles of the middle class against the medieval structures of feudalism and ecclesiastic domination. It is a fact that the modern mastery of the world through science and industry was accomplished more quickly among peoples and groups with a Protestant, and to be more exact a Reformed tradition, than it was in other places. From this fact the German social and economic historian Max Weber developed his famous thesis of the "congeniality" between *Calvinism and capitalism*. This thesis is disseminated by many today with the defamatory slogans that Calvinism is the "religion of capitalism" or that it mixes *Geist und Geld* (Spirit and money).

This contention however lacks any factual proof and Max Weber's thesis can scarcely hold up any longer historically. The actual figure whom Weber adduces to prove his theory is the American inventor and statesman Benjamin Franklin who lived from 1706 to 1790 in the period of mercantilism, that is, two hundred years after Calvin. In Franklin, Weber found maxims with religious and ethical overtones, such as: ceaseless work is an end in itself and the increase of capital is the highest aim. Weber thought he had detected the connection between religion and the accumulation of capital in the Calvinistic doctrine of unmerited election. It isolates man from society, deprives him of all sacramental and churchly mediations between himself and God, and makes him entirely dependent upon himself. How shall he become certain of his election? Since, according to the New Testament, only the good tree brings forth good fruit, the isolated soul must make itself certain of its election by constantly producing new good works. Good works are no longer a means to purchase one's salvation. Rather they are the means of ridding oneself of anxiety about one's salvation. Because one must constantly be able to see one's good works, the results of one's work may not be consumed, but must be capitalized.

Weber called this religious life-style, which he believed he had discovered in the Puritans of the seventeenth century, "inner worldly asceticism." In it Weber thought he recognized that spirit which has formed modern capitalism: the accumulation of capital through ascetic economizing. At the "cradle of the modern busi-nessman" stood the Puritan anxiously tending to his own election. Here were "bred those self-certain 'saints,' which we see again in the hard-as-steel Puritan merchants of the heroic periods of capi-talism and in individual examples down to the present." But as historical evidences Weber could cite only late Puritan texts, such as Richard Baxter's *Christian Directory or Body of Practical Divinity* (1673) and Richard Steele's *The Tradesman's Calling* (1684). And even from their writings he quoted only half the truth. He suppressed such themes as responsibility for the community, care for the weak, and education for the common good which are expressed in these pastoral writings and belonged to the reality of Puritan life.

Is there in the writings of Reformed theologians a recognizable connection between faith in election and zeal for business? Weber's thesis sounds quite plausible, but it cannot be supported by his-torical evidence. He himself excluded Calvin. According to Calvin, Christ is first and foremost the "mirror of election." In the knowl-edge of Christ's representative suffering and dying the believing person becomes sure of his call and election. There are for Calvin signs which accompany this, namely, the fear of God in one's heart and the community of the church which is gathered around the Word and the Lord's Supper. Calvin does not refer to the fruits of one's occupational labor. The Calvinist Synod of Dordrecht (1618) speaks of Christ as the revelation of God's election through grace, then of the self-witness of true, persevering faith, next of childlike fear of God and distress over one's sin, and only in the last place of zeal for a good conscience and good works. That these "good works" should consist of ceaseless work at one's job and the egoistic accumulation of capital is nowhere said, not even in the late Puritan literature of devotion and edification. Only the prosaic morality of a businessman in the Victorian period could speak in this way. An inner connection between Calvinist-Puritan faith in election and the spirit of capitalism cannot be demonstrated.

The history of the rise of capitalism is much more complex than Weber's one-dimensional thesis can account for. Capitalistic economic forms arose in the period of the Renaissance in the Lombardian cities. The business policies of the Fuggers, Welsers, Paumgartners, and other merchants belonging to the Catholic confession were clearly a form of "early capitalism." Even the mercantilist absolute princes, such as the Catholic Sun-King Louis XIV of France (1643–1715), may be described as "capitalistic." It may be the case that, in the eighteenth century, capitalistic forms of economy together with the first great industries developed faster in Protestant-Calvinist regions than elsewhere. But if this was so, it was due to the changed economic and geographical circumstances. The discovery of America and the sea routes to Asia had displaced the centers of trade to Northern and Western Europe. It has been shown that the predominance of Calvinism actually hindered rather than promoted capitalism in Geneva itself. In 1568 and again in 1580 the pastors successfully prevented the establishment of a bank.

But how did the Calvinist economic ethic appear if Max Weber's thesis cannot hold? The Reformation in Geneva was a renewal of faith but it included the whole life of the church, society, and politics. Calvin had a substantial part in refashioning the *ordre civil* (1543). He condemned the mercenary system and Genevan nationalism and he inspired a new openness toward refugees. With the establishment of the diaconate a new system of providing for the poor and the operation of hospitals was devised. Calvin took over from Luther the Reformation understanding of every worldly means of earning a livelihood as a *calling (Beruf)*. Whereas in the Middle Ages this word was reserved exclusively to the calling of the priests and the *vita contemplativa* stood higher than the *vita activa,* Luther and Calvin paved the way for a fundamentally new understanding of calling. In the "universal priesthood of all believers" every Christian has his calling. All work, in whatever calling, stands under the command and promise of God.

Precisely for this reason Calvin, in particular, persistently stressed the community-related character of one's vocational work. "Work is necessary so that all may live and it is to be done in such a way that there will be no exploitation of the poor by the rich, strangers by local citizens, the weak by the strong" (Max Geiger). Calvin followed the same tendency in his judgments about the *charging of interest.* Applying the Old Testament prophetic pronouncements against the taking of interest to his own situation, Calvin prohibited interest in the following case: no interest was to be taken from the poor. Capital investments which yield interest may be undertaken only insofar as they do not prejudice aid to those in need. Contracts for interest must be made according to the Golden Rule of Christ (Matt. 7:12).

Calvin set aside the rules of canon law and placed economic life under the command of God. Accordingly "the rights of the neighbor," especially of the weak and the fugitives, were decisive for him. In the economic ethic both of Calvin himself and of the Calvinist traditions one's work and possessions are to serve the neighbor, for "God is an advocate of the poor, the aliens, and the fugitives." The Reformed congregations have usually distinguished themselves through their exemplary social institutions and methods of caring for the poor. That capitalism in which every man preys like a wolf on every other man is utterly un-Calvinistic. In Germany the "Elberfelder system" of the Dutch Reformed congregations became a model for the state's welfare system. This was also the case in Switzerland, Holland, and England. The Calvinist economic ethic abandoned the class society of the old church; it did not, however, become the precursor of capitalism but rather of a just social order in freedom.

IV

In the political ethic of the Reformed churches the idea of the *religious covenant* and the theory of the *state contract* were predominant. Their long history of persecution and resistance gave rise to the idea of the right of popular resistance even by Christians to tyrannical authorities. From this idea was born the theological foundations of democracy. After the horrors of the Massacre of St. Bartholomew in Paris in 1572 Theodore von Beza, François

Hotman, and Hubert Languet developed a new theory of the
state and a political ethic. On the one hand, they reached back
to the "constitution" of the Holy Roman Empire, which was com-
posed of a variety of contracts and imperial capitulations, and,
on the other hand, they appropriated the Old Testament concept
of covenant. They replaced the hierarchical rule characteristic of
earlier conceptions of governing authority with the concept of
contract which became momentous for the whole of modernity:
God has made a double covenant with his people. The first covenant has been made by God with the whole people of God, who
promise allegiance to this covenant in the festival of covenant
renewal. Only on this foundation does there exist the particular
covenant which governs the actual distribution of political power
among the people, God, and the king. The authority of the king
derives from the sovereignty of the people as the people of God. If
he breaks the covenant, his authority reverts to the people, and
those who represent the people are authorized as well as obligated
to resistance. Because the covenant is made before God, one is
commanded to resist above all if the king violates the commands
of God or deserts to the enemies of God. This is resistance in
spiritual matters.

But it follows from this that the people are also justified in
resisting the king when he breaks his political agreements with
the people. This is resistance based on love for the neighbor. From
these biblical covenantal concepts there emerged the modern constitutional state which abolished rule by the nobility and the disposition to submissiveness. A prince who obstinately breaks the
mutual obligation of the covenant or the constitution is demon-
strably a tyrant. One must be more obedient to God than to such
an inhuman ruler. A people which breaks its obligation deriving
from this covenant must be considered seditious and should be
opposed.

Whereas for Luther rebellion in the Peasants' War was a greater
evil than tyranny, the Calvinists saw the misery of spiritual and
political tyranny more clearly and suffered from it in their own
bodies. By translating Luther's concept of the "universal priesthood of all believers" into the notion of the "universal kingship of
all believers," they became precursors of modern democracy. Not

only the king, but all men are defined by the image of God, said
John Milton. Therefore all people are created for lordship, not for
subjection. Thus a commonwealth of free men determines the
exercise of political power on the foundation of contracts. The
crown does not rest on the head of a man but on the constitution.
During the writing of the American Declaration of Independence
there was a long debate as to whether the constitution should be
called a "covenant" of a "constitution." This is an indication of
the extent to which the concept of covenant has worked its way
into modern constitutional history. It defines, limits, and controls
the practice of political rule by the people and their representatives, who are answerable to God alone.

There is in history only one Christian confession in which the
right of *resistance* has found a place. It is the Scottish Confession
of 1560. In its fourteenth article, which is an interpretation of the
Sixth Commandment, "You shall not commit murder," it is said
that one is "to represse tyrannie" and not "let innocent blude bee
sched." As the actions of John Knox and his friends show, this
meant not only passive but also active resistance, which under certain circumstances meets violence with violence.

Is this a Christian justification of violence from below? Active
resistance against demonstrable tyranny is, according to the Calvinist political ethic, nothing other than legitimate use of state
power. If a ruler breaks a contract, then the rule automatically
reverts to the people. The legitimacy of rule then lies on the side
of resistance against tyranny even if the tyrant controls the arsenal
of the state. To be obedient to God in the political order means
also to participate directly or indirectly in the practice of political
rule. Thus active resistance for the sake of the oppressed neighbor
is not only a right but also a duty of the Christian.

The way in which Calvinism bases the state and its constitution
theologically on the covenant with God and gives moral sanction
to the duty of resistance against the violation of that constitution
is more pertinent than ever to the contemporary political dilem-
mas which Christians face. German history could have developed
differently if the churches in Germany had adopted this political
ethic and had not cultivated the disposition to be submissive to
authority. The Reformed tradition outlines a relatively clear

course of action for the contemporary struggle against racist tyrannies of the world: if a government breaks its own laws, if it issues decrees which contradict its own constitution, if it sets up a constitution which stands in open contradiction to the "universal declaration of human rights," then there exists a clear case of tyranny which calls for legitimate resistance. The right of resistance is not based on ideological reasons, for instance, on the theory that democracy is an inherently better form of government. Resistance is called for, rather, in order to safeguard the rights of the neighbor and to protect the powerless.

WORKS FOR FURTHER STUDY

J. Bohatec, *Calvin und Bude: Studien zur Gedankenwelt des französischen Frühumanismus*, 1950; André Biéler, *The Social Humanism of Calvin*, trans. Paul T. Fuhrmann (Richmond: John Knox Press, 1964);

Jürgen Moltmann, *Prädestination und Perseveranz*, (Neukirchen: Neukirchener Verlag, 1961);

Max Weber, *The Protestant Ethic and the Spirit of Capitalism* (New York: Charles Scribner's Sons, 1958);

Max Geiger, "Calvin, Calvinismus, Kapitalismus," in *Gottesreich und Menschenreich. Ernst Staehlin zum 80. Geburtstag* (Basel: Helbing & Lichtenhahn, 1969);

G. Jellinek, *Die Erklärung der Menschen-und Bürgerrechte*, 1927[4];

J. T. McNeill, *The History and Character of Calvinism* (New York: Oxford University Press, 1958);

Karl Barth, *The Knowledge of God and the Service of God According to the Teaching of the Reformation* (London: Hodder and Stoughton, 1938).

X.

Racism and the Right to Resist

The decision of the World Council of Churches made in Arnoldshain in 1970 to start a program to combat racism and, among other
things, to give humanitarian aid to liberation movements in southern Africa marked a turning point for the ecumenical movement.[1]
For with that decision the World Council converted into deeds
the words against racism which it had been uttering with increasing sharpness since Evanston in 1954. In one sense, the unanimous
acceptance of the program by the Central Committee of the World
Council in Addis Ababa in 1971 brought to an end the debate
about the program itself.[2] However, the question of violence in
the context of the race problem remains to be thrashed out. The
World Council of Churches Central Committee called member
churches and Christians in all parts of the world to study violent
and nonviolent methods of social change, for—as the 1969 declaration of Canterbury says—"combating racism must entail a redistribution of social, economic, political, and cultural power from the
powerful to the powerless." Moreover, the Arnoldshain declaration has evoked many and varied negative reactions in the West
German churches, making an exercise in self-examination for us a
matter of urgency.

The process of conscientization which has now to begin is not
only related to the responsibility of the "donors" for the way in
which their money is used. Much more important would seem to
be the converse learning process. What can we learn about the
responsible use of power from the African Christians who are
resisting racism either passively or actively? Without an understanding of such resistance as a Christian duty, and without personal readiness to resist in comparable situations, the necessary
solidarity cannot develop. Donations can be a token; but basically
Christians in those countries do not need white solicitude or

champions to defend them; they need brothers who understand them. The "problem of violence" cannot therefore be narrowed down to a question of whom and what we can support, but comes back to ourselves.

The negative reactions in West Germany have revealed a confused attitude toward power in the German traditions as well as a Christian repression complex as regards resistance against tyranny. From ancient times our political conscience has maintained that a conserving violence must be endorsed in preference to a liberating violence and that the power of government, even when used unlawfully and unjustly, is preferable to active resistance against it. Better a tyrannical government than revolution is the watchword in the country of the many abortive revolutions. Admittedly in our churches everywhere after the Second World War there was a searching discussion about resistance to Hitler, the July 20th plot and the road taken by Bonhoeffer. The insights gained from that discussion have obviously vanished and have been thrust to the back of our minds. In any case they were simply not in evidence in recent months during the argument about the use of violence in combating racism. For lack of self-knowledge and because people had repressed their awareness of such problems dating from the time of the dictatorship in Germany, there was failure to understand the resistance of black Christians in countries with racial dictatorships. Let us try to talk about today's burning question, "What is your attitude to violence?", without anger or passion, for there is no reason to repress it or to react allergically to it.

By racism we mean ethnocentric *pride* in one's own racial group and preference for the distinctive characteristics of that goup; belief that these characteristics are fundamentally biological in nature and are thus transmitted to succeeding generations; strong negative feelings toward other groups who do not share these characteristics coupled with the thrust to discriminate against and exclude the outgroup from full participation in the life of the community.[3]

This racism is not limited to particular countries today. It is a world problem. White racism in former colonial countries, where slaves used to be kept, is certainly not the only variety. There is also colored racism in India, Indonesia, and Africa, as there is xenophobia to be found everywhere. Nevertheless, white and colored racism are not on a par (as the statement of the Council of the Evangelical Church in Germany on September 24, 1970 seems to assume). White racism is by far the most dangerous form of racism, because through it social, economic, and political power structures are organized and defended, which contradict the Universal Declaration of Human Rights. In such countries racism is not simply an ethnic group phenomenon, but an instrument of domination which secures political, economic, and cultural privileges for the whites and makes second-class human beings of black and colored people, unless they can be designated "honorary whites" like the economically powerful Japanese. For this reason, the race question here cannot be solved solely by a change in the individual conscience but only by a change in the racist power structures, in order to achieve a redistribution of power from the powerful to the powerless. Conversely, however, such a redistribution of power will not be achieved unless people get rid of the racist mentality, any more than the institutional abolition of slavery in the Southern states of the United States a hundred years ago really eliminaed the racist mentality of many whites there. Racism is in this connection both a form of ideology and a manifestation of the institutions of power.[4]

For a long time the United Nations has spoken out against racist dictatorships on the grounds of their violations of elementary human rights, and called on member states to boycott them economically. Some years ago, the British Commonwealth decided to impose economic sanctions against Rhodesia and South Africa. These measures have proved ineffective. Among the whites in those countries there has long been a liberal Christian minority working for the eventual improvement, without violence, of the situation of the blacks. It has had to endure many repressive measures and to make many sacrifices. This minority, as well as the blacks and even the supporters of the policy of apartheid, are all agreed that, instead of improving, the situation has in recent years worsened, so that the hope for nonviolent change has diminished.

THE SHIFT TO COUNTERVIOLENCE

The African liberation fronts of today emphasize that they grew out of nonviolent groups. At the beginning of the 1950s, Albert

Luthuli was President of the African National Congress (ANC).[5] As a Christian he supported the principles of nonviolent resistance and wanted to lead his people to freedom on the model of Gandhi. At the beginning, the method used was that of civil disobedience against laws which were contrary to human rights. The government reacted with special laws and fines, imprisonment, and flogging. In 1964, Nelson Mandela, Luthuli's successor, said:

We of ANC had always stood for a nonracial democracy, and we shrank from any policy which might drive the races even further apart than they already were. But the hard facts were that fifty years of nonviolence had brought African people nothing but more and more repressive legislation, and fewer rights.[6]

This was the reason for the founding of the militant resistance movement "Spear of the Nation." Nonviolent resistance had been misconstrued as the green light for violent action against the blacks.

In 1964, the ecumenical consultation in Mindolo recognized for the first time the inevitability of the use of counterviolence after the failure of the many nonviolent attempts to change the situation. Many African leaders maintain that there would never have been any desire to use violence if any other effective forms of action could have been found or had remained open. In 1966, the Conference on Church and Society in Geneva had this to say on the subject:

It is not enough for churches and groups to condemn the sin of racial arrogance and oppression. The struggle for radical change in structures will inevitably bring suffering and will demand costly and bitter engagement.

Eduardo Mondlane, the black Christian from Mozambique, who had been a professor at the University of Syracuse in the state of New York, was present at this conference. He entered into this "costly and bitter engagement," became the organizer of FRELIMO and died in 1969 in Dar-es-Salaam, the victim of a bomb attack. Since then, ecumenical conferences and statements have not condemned the victims of racism who have been forced by necessity to turn to violence, but have recognized their engagement. The use of revolutionary counterviolence in racist dictatorships remains a "bitter engagement," it is true. Yet without participation in power and in economic and political decision-making, the just struggle of the oppressed for identity and dignity cannot be achieved. A redistribution of power presupposes participation in power, and where this is notoriously and violently refused, counterviolence is often the only remedy.

There is no word of approval of violence in the World Council's resolution. Only an unscrupulous press brought the question of violence, immediately after the meeting in Arnoldshain, to the notice of the horrified German public: "No church funds to buy machine guns for guerrillas"! The resolution spoke only of humanitarian aid. The World Council did not, however, reserve to itself control of the money but, for reasons dictated by conscience, placed confidence in the assurances of the organizations concerned that they would use the money for the purposes for which it was given. Because of this, the organization "Brot für die Welt" (Bread for the World) and a few church leaders hastened to dissociate themselves publicly from any support of violent action. Unfortunately, the letter from Bishop Dietzfelbinger, Chairman of the Council of the Evangelical Church in Germany, gave prominence to the question of violence, by expressing the suspicion that:

in the case of at least some of the organizations being supported the question arises whether the terms of this service are still being respected, namely, to support nonviolent measures consonant with the purposes of the World Council of Churches.

Now a few questions do arise in connection with the restriction to "humanitarian aid." First, since the civil war in Nigeria/Biafra, in which incomparably larger sums were sent to Biafra through the churches, it has been clear that aid to hospitals and schools can indirectly mean political support and thus, still more indirectly, strengthen military potential. It is "impossible" to make a hard and fast distinction between money which one and the same organization gives for a number of purposes," said Mikko Juva,

President of the Lutheran World Federation. Second, if the crux of the racist problem is the "redistribution of power from the powerful to the powerless," then "purely humanitarian aid" has only limited value in solving the problem. Third, even if it is only churches over there which are supported by churches here, as the Lutheran Church leaders proposed, the funds nevertheless do support the fight against racism, through those churches which have taken sides in the fight. Nevertheless, the restriction to humanitarian aid has its good side, for the aid supports the liberation movements in their struggle against racism, with no political strings attached. The movements are left to judge for themselves what, in such situations, is humane and humanitarian. The restriction to humanitarian aid was wise, as it gives evidence of confidence, while avoiding political tutelage.

However, the letter from Bishop Dietzfelbinger and the statement to the churches by the Council of the Evangelical Church in Germany equated this with the "principle of nonviolence," which is "consonant with the gospel." We ought therefore to examine whether the principle of nonviolence, and nonviolence as a principle in political and social arguments, is in fact consonant with the gospel, and to what extent reliance on this principle can help the oppressed. As aid to Biafra showed, it is difficult to draw a clear dividing line. Our churches themselves exist in the political arena, together with their installations, legal rights, and resources, and they are political factors with which every politician reckons. Nor is it easy to declare that nonviolence should be the principle of others, while at the same time expressing the belief that military service is a possibility for Christians. On this question, double standards are absolutely barred. Such is also the view of Helmut Gollwitzer who writes: "Anyone who uses pacifist arguments on the question of revolution but not on the question of the army reveals his argument as the ideology of the ruling class."[7] Nonviolence in the solution of social and political problems is only possible in areas where power is more or less absent and these are rare on this earth. However, the principle of nonviolence can provide desirable criteria on which to base political action involving the use of force.

The concept of nonviolence belongs to the eschatological remembrance of faith in Jesus. The hoped-for kingdom of God is the kingdom of brotherhood without violence and in this sense "anarchy" (Berdyaev). This explains the Christian's deep horror of violence already in the present. He does not want to be master of any slaves or the slave of any master and will do his best to create and extend spheres of communication that are free of domination. He will also give preference to nonviolent methods in political disputes. In the domain of politics, however, it is a question of power, distribution of power, and participation in the exercise of power. "We are here to deal with church and state, so to speak, on the edge of the church in the sphere of the world not yet redeemed. To live in this world and to obey God in it is to take part in the use of violence directly or indirectly."[8]

Thus we cannot start from a "principle of nonviolence" but must justify the use of power in view of the desired brotherhood without violence. To achieve this, it is important to settle the exact meaning of the words *violence, power,* and *domination,* for in general not very clear distinctions are drawn between them, as is shown by the quotations and text of this article. The word *violence* already suggests undertones of abuse of power and is not usually applied to the legitimate and legal exercise of power. The word *power* is more appropriate here. By "power" we designate the means by which we can obtain something by force. The *law* lays down the rules which we must follow in gaining acceptance of our claims. The use of power must therefore be by lawful means; otherwise it is injustice, despotism, outrage, terror, brutality—in other words, violence. The rights must however be *just* and may not make injustice the norm. The *legitimacy* of a country's laws and political decisions is determined by the constitution of the country, wherein the basic rights of the citizens are formulated and laid down. These basic rights must in turn be consonant with the Universal Declaration of Human Rights (1948), if it is claimed that a country's constitution is based on justice and humanity.

The so-called problem of violence is not one of alternatives—violence or nonviolence—but of criteria which should govern the justifiable or unjustifiable use of power.[9] Justified "violence" can be called power. The unjustified exercise of power is then naked violence. Throughout its long history, Christianity has been the instrument by which the theory that "power can do no wrong" has been demolished in our countries. Power does not come from the right of the stronger or the struggle for existence, but must be publicly justified. Precisely because love demands that all domination and violence be eliminated, the exercise of power needs justification. Where does violence exist today in the sense of the unjust exercise of power, involving violation of the law as well as unconstitutional laws and constitutions which are contrary to the Declaration of Human Rights?

RESISTANCE TO TYRANTS

If we ask questions of this kind, we come up against the military dictatorships and then the racial dictatorships. The question of the "injured and the insulted" (Dostoevsky) is not one of "violence or nonviolence" but of submission to unjust and unlawful violence or of counterviolence which liberates from unlawful violence and creates a lawful, constitutional situation, consonant with human rights. Naturally, in a democratic society there would be ways and means of achieving better justice by other methods. But in this case action has to be taken not in democratic but in dictatorial and terrorist situations.

We are coming one step closer to the problem of the use of counterviolence, when we take up the question which has been debated by Christians from the very beginning—whether we have the right to resist tyranny.[10] In early Germanic legal concepts—which are, incidentally, similar to the early African tribal constitution—the relationship between ruler and people was determined by mutual loyalty and not merely by obedience. In the "Sachsenspiegel" (III, § 78, 2) we find: "A man must also resist his king and judge when the latter does wrong and even help to restrain him in every way, whether or not he is that man's liege-lord. To do so does not constitute a breach of trust." On the basis of the Christian teaching on natural law, the church in the Middle Ages adopted and legitimized this right to resist and in so doing conceived itself to be the authentic interpreter of the natural law. According to Thomas Aquinas, tyranny can be degenerate authority (*tyrannis exercitio*, "somewhat outside of legality") as well as usurped authority (*tyrannis ex defectu titulo*). Both run counter to the values of peace, justice, and order. Those who had entered into an engagement with the liege-lord were entitled to resist actively; they were normally the estates and, in the case of an elected monarchy, the electors. According to Thomas Aquinas, in the extreme case of tyranny following the usurpation of power, tyrannicide was permissible.

REVOLUTIONARY DUTY OF CHRISTIANS

This is not the place to recapitulate the whole history of the right to resist. Under different forms of government it takes correspondingly different forms. In the course of the democratization of forms of government, the right to resist was finally transferred from the estates to the citizens, who guaranteed their political union in the constitution. Since the American and French constitutions at the end of the eighteenth century, human rights have, with increasingly binding force, become the criterion of the legitimate exercise of power and legitimate resistance.

Luther viewed resistance in extreme cases in very different ways. For him resistance was often linked with the concept of lawless insurrection. However, in consideration of the threat to Protestant countries and cities from the counter reformers, the Hapsburg "universal" monarchy, he agreed with the arguments of Protestant jurists and of Melanchthon. There were the Schmalkaldic League and the Schmalkaldic War. In the Peasants' War, Luther stated that a Christian ought not to obey an unlawful command, but, at the same time, he must do nothing to endanger the government, which was ordained by God. When compared with insurrection and anarchy, the degeneration of government into tyranny seemed to him the lesser evil. Only in the extreme case, where total denial of rights and arbitrary despotism take over, does Luther acknowledge a divine command to resist. Luther saw in this situation the apocalyptic vision of the eschatological tyrants (2 Thess. 2:7ff.). Mostly he identified the anti-Christ with the abuse of spiritual power in the Papacy, yet he did see that there might also be political tyrants. He recognized that "Christians had a revolutionary duty" to combat both.[11]

In the years of the political and ideological dictatorship in Germany and, through Germany, in Europe, many Christians and churches in Europe attached themselves to movements of either passive or active resistance. From this experience there followed after the war the attempt to change the submissive attitude of German Protestantism. Karl Barth took up for consideration Article XIV of the Scottish Confession, according to which obedience to the commandment "Thou shalt not kill" also requires that Christians should "repress tyranny" (*tyrannidem opprimere*). This task is part of the duty to love one's neighbor: "to save the lives of innocents, to repress tyranny, to defend the oppressed." The spilling of innocent blood should never be tolerated if it can be avoided. Resistance in circumstances where political power is abused—if necessary by the use of violence—is a commandment in the context of responsibility for one's neighbor and the state. Barth commented:

In such a situation must not faith in Jesus Christ active in love necessitate our active resistance in just the same way as it necessitates passive resistance or our positive cooperation, when we are not faced with this choice?[12]

Addressing the Lutheran World Federation Assembly in 1952, the Norwegian Lutheran Bishop Eivind Berggrav said:

When a government becomes lawless and acts with arbitrary despotism, the result is a demonic condition, that is to say, the government is godless. To obey such a Satanic government would be nothing short of sinful. . . . In circumstances of this kind, we have as a matter of principle the right to rebel in one form or another.

LEGITIMATION OF RESISTANCE

In the case of obvious and proven tyranny, there is theological backing, based on Christianity, for the right and obligation to resist. Tyranny is proven where there is: (1) continuous violation of law; (2) violation of the constitution; and (3) violation of human rights which is itself legalized by laws and constitutions. Passive and active resistance in such cases is not "insurrection" or "terrorism" but legitimate use of justified political power and, for Christians, it is normal political participation in abnormal circumstances. However, the resistance must itself be legitimized, either: (1) by restoration of legality; (2) by restoration of the constitution;

or (3) by a new constitution in which human rights are recognized as the basic rights of the citizens.

Let us assume that in the case of tyranny in one form or another there is both justified and lawful resistance; then we are faced with the problem of conscience in regard to the use of force, for those attempting to substitute a lawful state of affairs for tyrannical injustice are themselves obliged to use counterviolence in contravention of the values which they desire to embody in the new constitution. Yet we ought not to make resistance the only touchstone in this matter of conscience, and certainly not wait to do so until it is a question of active resistance. If the resistance is legitimate, then it is a matter of the exercise of legitimate political power. Resistance is not the equivalent of a state of war, but is legitimate defense in a civil war which tyrants or a tyrannical class of people have begun against the rest of the population in order to make slaves of the citizens—for example, to make "second-class human beings" of black people. The problem of conscience associated with active resistance is therefore basically none other than the problem of conscience associated with a government's normal exercise of power and the participation therein of Christians. Of course, active resistance does represent quite a different burden on conscience. However, anyone who approves of the normal exercise of power by the state for the sake of love as unavoidable or who is not a pacifist in the fundamental, anarchical sense cannot suddenly make resistance an extreme case of conscience. Anyone who holds up to those engaged in active resistance the principle of nonviolence as being consonant with the gospel, but who does not do so whenever the state exercises power, confuses people's conscience.

Nevertheless, it is naturally difficult for the resistance to a situation of legalized disorder, injustice, and terror to act lawfully and without using terrorist methods. Understandably, the danger of letting the more powerful opponent dictate the battlefield and the weapons and of practicing only revenge instead of greater justice, is always very present. What form should lawful and legitimate resistance take in a country where the police lawlessly torture and liquidate persons and the courts are corrupt? It is not possible in every case for the people's counter government to introduce legal proceedings; instead, immediate active intervention by phys-

ical force is called for. In situations of this kind, how should the
legality of the activities of the resistance be established? In manuals
of ethics this problem is often dealt with as a borderline case. For
example: if the driver of a bus carrying a full load of passengers
suddenly goes mad and heads for a precipice, the only thing to do
for the protection of the passengers, if anyone can manage to do
it, is to render the driver harmless and wrench the steering wheel
out of his hand. Regardless of whether anything of this kind has
ever happened, it is clear from the example that killing remains
killing and as such cannot be justified. However, in such a situation it will probably be unavoidable and in a theological sense the
guilt of the man who did the killing can be forgiven. Guilt remains
guilt, even if the man was quite unable to act otherwise, because
doing nothing would have meant being responsible for the deaths
of many people. In itself then, such an act of violence cannot be
approved, but it can be answered for. Responsible action in
such cases demands a love that is ready to incur guilt in order to
save. This is only possible in the awareness that all action in
history is dependent on forgiveness (Eduard Heimann).

Albert Camus dealt with this problem of conscience under the
title "The Fastidious Assassins"[13] and referred to those Russian
assassins who refused to explode the carriage of the Grand Duke
because they knew that children were in the carriage. They were
clear in their own minds that the murder of tyrants, which they
considered necessary, so contradicted the humanity which they were
attempting to represent that they had to be prepared for suicide
or for execution.

Dietrich Bonhoeffer called the structure of responsible action
"the readiness to incur guilt":

Jesus took upon himself the guilt of all men, and for that reason every
man who acts responsibly becomes guilty. If any man tries to escape
guilt in responsibility . . . [he] cuts himself off from the redeeming
mystery of Christ's bearing guilt without sin and he has no share in the
divine justification. . . . He sets his own personal innocence above his
responsibility for men, and he is blind to the more irredeemable guilt
which he incurs precisely in this; he is blind also to the fact that real
innocence shows itself precisely in a man's entering into the fellowship
of guilt for the sake of other men.[14]

VIOLENCE IN THE CONTEXT OF LOVE

It is not the idealistic principle of nonviolence that is consonant with the gospel, but the responsible action of love. Love is divine power-in-weakness (2 Cor. 12:9). Responsible political action in love is selfless to the point of sacrifice of personal innocence, to the point of incurring guilt. From this we are led to the following conclusions: first, nonviolence in the sense of nonresistance cannot be justified in tyrannical situations, because it permits and encourages violence. It does not save the personal innocence of the individual, but leads to "more irredeemable guilt." Second, violence, construed as the love which desires to put an end to evil, cannot be approved but it can be answered for. Resistance may not triumph over its victims. It is revenge, not love, which does that. Guilt remains guilt, but in faith we can live with this guilt and need not commit suicide. The engagement to resist remains a "bitter engagement." But in this instance too the incurring of guilt in the responsible love which has recourse to counterviolence cannot be restricted to the case of resistance. It is only that the example of resistance reveals the factors which, secretly and often unconsciously, determine all political action. Third, it follows from this that action and failure to act are not the same in such situations in the sense that either way one incurs guilt. There is the "more irredeemable guilt" which in most cases consists of sins of omission.

NO SEPARATION BETWEEN CHURCH AND CHRISTIANS

Lastly, there comes the question of whether the resistance described above and its support from outside is the concern of Christians and, if it is the concern of Christians, whether it can then be the concern of the church. Here doubt arises about inherited religious concepts in our tradition.

Some people claim that the church's task is simply to preach the Word of God and not to recommend action that belongs to the political sphere. Again, the decision of the World Council is construed as a sign of the apocalyptic incursion of evil into the church, and there is a demand for the true church of Jesus to be separated from the political church of Barabbas, since Barabbas was a Jewish freedom-fighter. Dictators have often been and still are politically supported by this "unpolitical" attitude. The separation of faith and love, of persons and conditions, implicit in this attitude, has no foundation in Christianity.

There are those who say that, of course, racism and racist power-structures are contrary to the gospel, and that for this reason it is the duty of Christians to support the resistance whenever they are in a position to do so. These people add, however, that the church as an institution cannot do this, for it cannot in the name of its members make a political decision with which many of these members do not approve. This separation between the institutional church and the individual Christian finds no support in the New Testament and is contrary to the "Theology of the Word of God," according to which the beliefs of the individual and the church itself are *creaturae verbi*. Moreover, it is impractical, because individuals always act in groups and in interaction with groups and institutions. By such a separation, the gospel is neutralized, so that its salt cannot come to earth.

Between the dreaded tutelage by the church over its members' political conscience and the alleged individual nature of political decisions, there lies a whole series of possibilities for achieving a consensus and joint action; only those churches which separate church and politics in the old established church way are unaware of these possibilities.

No Christian can dispute that racism is "contrary to the Gospel and incompatible with the Christian doctrine of man and with the nature of the Church of Christ" (Evanston, 1954), and thus that racism constitutes a "blatant denial of the Christian faith" (Uppsala, 1968). On this basis, W. A. Visser't Hooft, in a speech at Uppsala, called racism a "moral heresy." If we take these statements seriously, then it follows that it is not only doubt about the spiritual mandate of the church and its teaching which must be called heretical, but also disavowals of the temporal mandate of the church and finally racist structures in the churches themselves. If this is correct, then we have to reckon with self-excommunication or with excommunication by the church and with schism within the church on this question. In the past churches have often excluded orthodox Christians because of their private moral sins.

In the United States there were also churches which excommuni-
cated slave-owners, even though the latter adhered to all the articles of the Christian faith. Because of the race questions whole
churches have in recent years cut themselves off from the World
Council of Churches. As in the case of doctrinal decisions, one
must reckon with schisms in the case of important decisions in
practical life.

But how can the political responsibility of Christians be organized as a responsibility of the church? If we recognize only the
large institution and the individual members, then it cannot be
organized except by the use of circular letters intended to awaken
the individual's awareness of problems. There are, however, within
the church—between the institution and the individuals—an
abundance of intermediate social groupings and of opportunities
to create groups and to build up a common will.

Finally, there are the synods whose assignment, according to their
name ("synod"), is to explore and follow the "path of common action." Churches which are organized on a presbyterial and synodal
basis have often found the common political path in situations that
were relatively unambiguous politically. The problems which have
arisen in West German Evangelical churches in connection with
the anti-racism program show that the churches need to develop
a new understanding of the church in theory and practice alike.
The church is not only an *institution* for the preaching of the
Word and the administration of the sacraments. It is also the concrete *community of the faithful,* and as the concrete community
of the faithful the church is also the practical *community of love.*
In its mission in and to the world, Christianity is in this third
respect a living thing. The consensus must be achieved, in the form
of community building, on what is called in the specific case "love"
in politics and society. Support for anti-racism funds from money
derived from church taxes can be obtained by synodal decision,
the comparative voting figures being published. Support can also
be achieved through voluntary self-taxation as a church project.
Lastly it can be indirectly encouraged by an analysis and criticism
of the political existence of the church and its financial policy,
through which, as a result of the economic involvement of our country with the racist countries, those power structures are maintained.

The way taken by the World Council of Churches does not mean that instead of being an organization of churches it has confined its life to the sphere of international politics, nor does it mean disintegration of the Christian faith into revolutionary movements. It is a road that leads to a growth of awareness of the political existence and the political responsibility of the church of the Son of man in an inhuman world. The African freedom movements and the Christians in them are asking crucial questions of our churches and about our own existence as Christians. Not until we have heard those questions and pondered the problems of resistance in situations of tyranny—problems which we have repressed in our consciousness—shall we be in a position to ask crucial questions of them. Not only development aid and anti-racist programs are on the agenda but the development of ecumenical solidarity in political and social responsibility.

NOTES TO CHAPTER TEN

1. *Evangelische Kommentare* (1971): 45–49, 105–108.
2. S. M. Daecke, "Reform-Racismus-Religionen," *Evangelische Kommentare* (1971): 145–148.
3. *Uppsala Spricht* (Geneva, 1968), p. 68.
4. Cf. H. W. Florian, *Violence in Southern Africa* (London: SCM, 1970), p. 21.
5. Albert Luthuli, *Mein Land–Mein Leben* (Munich: Chr. Kaiser, 1961).
6. H. W. Florian, *Violence in Southern Africa*, p. 32.
7. *Diskussion zur "Theologie der Revolution,"* ed. E. Feil and R. Weth (Munich: Chr. Kaiser, 1969), p. 61.
8. K. Barth, *The Knowledge of God and the Service of God According to the Teaching of the Reformaiton*, trans. J. L. M. Haire and I. Henderson (London: Hodder and Stoughton, 1938), p. 231. (Translation slightly altered.)
9. Cf. J. Moltmann, "God in Revolution," in *Religion, Revolution, and the Future*, trans. M. Douglas Meeks (New York: Charles Scribner's Sons, 1969), Thesis 6, pp. 143–145; also S. M. Daecke in the above-mentioned report on the Conference in Addis Ababa.
10. Ernst Wolf, "Widerstandsrecht," in *Religion in Geschichte und Gegenwart*, 3d ed., vol. IV, pp. 1681–1690.
11. Ibid., p. 1686.
12. K. Barth, *Knowledge of God*, p. 230.
13. A. Camus, *The Rebel: An Essay in Man in Revolt*, trans. Anthony Bower (New York: Vintage Books, 1956), pp. 164–173.
14. D. Bonhoeffer, *Ethics*, ed. E. Bethge, trans. N. H. Smith (New York: Macmillan, 1965), p. 241.

XI.

The Theological Basis of Human Rights and of the Liberation of Human Beings

I. THE CURRENT SITUATION

From its inception the ecumenical movement has been conscious of its connection with political movements for the international recognition of human rights. "We observe with pleasure the development of an international awareness of responsibility for the respect of human rights" (First General Assembly of the Lutheran World Federation, Lund, 1947). Session IV, Art. 17–22, of the Fourth General Assembly of the World Council of Churches in Uppsala, expressly acknowledged

that the development of social justice in all human relationships presupposes that human dignity is recognized and protected and that the full equality of men of all races and nations as well as of the adherents of all religions and ideologies will become the common goal of the community of nations. (Art. 17)

The Fifth General Assembly of the Lutheran World Federation in Evian, France (1970) took the following stand: "The churches should be summoned to search for ways, means, and opportunities of enabling their members to study the *Universal Declaration of Human Rights* and to undertake the application of this declaration in the national life of their member churches." Articles 1, 5, 9, 10, 18, 19, and 26 were explicitly cited. It is therefore time to think through in a fundamental way the theological basis of human rights so that this summons does not remain a declaration to which we are not really bound.

The *political and social directions of the churches gain* their *universal significance* only in their relationship to human rights. With regard to human rights, the church necessarily becomes the "church for others" or the "church for the world." The decision of the World Council of Churches in Arnoldshain, September, 1970, arising out of this understanding of the church, to give public and financial support to the anti-racism program has its basis in a theology of human rights. It aroused resistance and confusion precisely because many member churches have neglected to study human rights. In opposition to the resolutions we have mentioned they have considered these concerns alien to their task as the church. They did not recognize, nor did they want to recognize, the Christian character of the declarations of human rights.

What theological relevance do declarations of human rights have for the political and social practice of Christianity in the world? What relevance does the political and social existence of the church have for the spreading and the realization of human rights?

II. THE HISTORY OF THE DECLARATION OF HUMAN RIGHTS

Cultural anthropology has pointed out that the perception and acknowledgment of *man* is a rather recent phenomenon. There were cultures in which the term *man* was reserved exclusively for the members of one's own tribe; strangers were not viewed as men. In its primitive form this *ethnocentrism* has its roots in the fact that early languages knew only few abstract concepts. In these languages there are palms, cedars, and oaks but not yet the inclusive concept *tree*. Thus there are fellow tribesmen and strangers but as yet no word for common humanity. Psychology has demonstrated that the present-day refusal to recognize others as men happens intentionally. War propaganda notoriously makes enemies subhuman: Jews, Russians, Japs, gooks, niggers, communists, miserable dogs, etc. They are the barbarians who are known only as enemies and may live only as slaves. Thus men identify humanity with the positives they possess; race, caste, class, religion, etc., and project the inhuman, which they want to repress in themselves, onto the stranger who is different. Self-assertion and declassification of the other, self-justification and hatred of the strangers, are nourished by the demonic compulsion of man to self-affirmation.

The concept of *humanitas,* which is common to Greeks and barbarians, emerges in our cultural sphere in the philosophy of the Sophists and the Stoics. All men are equals on the basis of their common human nature. Their distinctions are determined merely externally and historically. The common human nature is self-evident by virtue of the inborn ideal of reason which is common to all. Cicero placed over against the ancient Roman idea of *homo romanus* the higher ideal of *homo humanus.* The corresponding antithesis is therefore no longer Romans or barbarians, free man or slave, but human or inhuman among Romans and barbarians, among free men or slaves.

Where, in other cultural spheres, are there comparable developments of the concept of humanity?

Another concept of humanity parallel to this emerged from the biblical traditions. Adam was not the first Jew but the first man. If God the Creator fashioned man in his *image* on earth, then the inner dignity, freedom, and responsibility of *man* extends impartially beyond every human community and state organization. It is not *a* king, as in the ideology of the pharaohs, but *man,* who is the image of God on earth. If God acts as the liberator of man in an inhuman history, then the goal of Israel as well as of Christianity is the new, just humanity of God. The historical monotheism of the Old Testament leads logically to the notion of one humanity. Before God, all individual destinies and national histories merge into a single and common world history. The late Israelite expectation of the coming kingdom of the Son of man (Daniel 7), which will overcome the "beastly kingdoms of the world," and the Christian proclamation of Jesus as the Son of man and the new man display a theological and *future-oriented concept of humanity.* Here it is not a question of a common human nature knitting together different men. Rather their common definition in terms of the similitude of God and their common future in the coming kingdom of God bind them together in such a way that their historical differences are to be overcome. "Every valley shall be lifted up, and every mountain and hill be made low"; so that "all flesh together" can see the glory of the Lord (Isa. 40:4, 5).

Only in the sixteenth century do human rights emerge as instruments in the political struggle for the legal security of the individual against the coercion of the state. Their development is not yet finished.

The Christianization of the European states transformed the relationship of man to the state in a twofold manner. (1) If man is God's image, he is a responsible person and bearer of the rights and duties of freedom (Boethius: *rationalis naturae individua substantia*). Man does not exist for the sake of the state, but the state for the sake of man. (2) The state is therefore no longer "God on earth," but has to respect and guard the dignity of man. With this, human rights become the *basic rights* of state constitutions. Basic rights are the standards by which civil rights and state power must be criticized and judged. That state power is not taken for granted, but must be justified, is a result of the Christianization of these states.

Yet the religious and theoretical right of human freedom (in faith and before God) and factual, social and political unfreedom remained intertwined throughout the Middle Ages. Basically only the *nobles* secured privileges for themselves by means of contracts with monarchs (e.g., the *Magna Charta Liberatum,* 1215). They brought into our history, however, the notion of the *state contract* through which political power became limited and controllable. On this ground English Puritanism developed the *Rights of Parliament* in the *Petition of Rights* (1628) and the *Bill of Rights* (1689). The protective aspect of human rights was developed at this point in time: guarantee against illegal incarceration, guarantee of religious freedom, etc. Only with the American *Declaration of the Rights of Virginia* (1776) was that government or state contract finally ruled legal by constitution. The constitution or covenant understands human rights "as the basis and foundation of government." "All men are by nature equally free and independent, and have certain inherent rights. . . ." These rights are seen as self-evident axioms of every human policy. Yet in this declaration of the foundations of the constitution a specific declaration of intention is missing with regard to the concrete distinctions between rights and property among whites and slaves, among rich and poor.

In the first article of the French Constitution of 1791 such an intention is more concretely stressed. "Men are born free and equal in rights and remain so. Social differences can be grounded only on the common needs." The *droit de l'homme* is translated into the *droit du citoyen*. In the nineteenth century the middle class, which had borne the human rights movement, more and more renounced the intention of emancipation of man from rule and inequality and increasingly stressed the protective side of the state for the guaranteeing of stability to human rights and individual freedoms.

Out of the Russian Revolution arose a constitution of the exploited against the exploiters. Article three of the *Constitution of the Russian Socialist Federated Congress of Republics* (1918), includes these words: "in struggle to destroy every exploitation of man by man, every class division of society, unmercifully to crush the exploiters. . . ." Also the *Constitution of the Union of Soviet Socialist Republics* (1936) calls rights which merely preserve the state no protection against state encroachments. The state constitution is here essentially severed from the tradition of middle-class human rights.

The Fascist terror in Europe led in the West to the Atlantic Charter in 1941, and after the war to the establishment of the United Nations (San Francisco, 1945), whose Universal Declaration of Human Rights (1948) is recognized up to the present as the internationally binding statement of human rights. Because of the experiences of tyranny, the protective side of the state vis-à-vis the human rights allegedly under its care is obviated. It represents social demands which go beyond the middle-class limitation to individual freedoms. Finally, the future character of human rights is emphasized. After the preamble "the General Assembly proclaims the Universal Declaration of Rights which is before us as the common ideal to be attained by all peoples and nations. . . ." It contains therefore not only a declaration of the basis but also a declaration of intent. But how we are to get from this ideal to its practical realization remains unexplained because the United Nations lacks the power for realization. Since then, however, human rights have won an international character and are not openly disputed by any nation.

III.   THEOLOGICAL PROBLEMS OF HUMAN RIGHTS

Human rights have issued out of the process of the Christianization of societies and states. The vital dignity of the human person as an object of concern has taken shape in legal and political institutions. The actual liberation and the experienced freedom of man have already been realized in laws and institutions of freedom. The process of Christianization exists between church life specifically and political life in general. Whether they work in evolutionary or revolutionary ways, the present struggles for a better humanity and a more radical liberation must find their bearings in relation to these processes. Otherwise they are in the air and without relationship to anything. The revolution of freedom also knows the tradition of freedom and has to take it up into itself.

The well-known declarations of human rights we have mentioned, however, are effective only insofar as there are men who are prepared to take upon themselves the rights and duties of men and stand up for the oppressed for the sake of humanity. The rights of freedom are effective only insofar as there are free men who intercede for the liberation of enslaved men. The question is whether and to what extent present-day living Christianity actualizes a reality for humanity and freedom which fills these human rights with social and political life.

Two principal questions can be posed to the Universal Declaration of Human Rights:

What functions can this declaration serve? It can be understood as a *universal fundament* of various national constitutions. The several civil rights are then derived from the basic rights of man and must be judged by them. But in the case of conflict, who or what takes precedence: human rights as related to fundamental rights or national security?

It can be understood, in the second place, as a *common ideal* of the nations. Then the fundamental intention of the declaration of human rights is a society of humanity on earth in which the egoism of national foreign policy is eliminated and replaced by a mutual world domestic policy. But in the case of conflict, who or what takes precedence: the desired society of humanity or the interest of one's own nation?

Whether understood as universal fundament or as universal ideal of separate nations, the weaknesses of human rights exist in the fact that there are too few powers for realizing them over against injustice and oppression. They can very easily be misused as the intellectual facade of evil. Often, fundamental declarations have a mere decorative character and in actuality serve the concealment of the opposite. How much unfreedom is there in the "free world"? How much unbrotherliness is there in the "socialist world"? Ideals, if one takes them seriously, can change reality. But they can also become the mere justification of good intentions, without a corresponding will for realization. It is really a matter then of clarifying the *relationship of the theory of human rights to* practice in order to exclude misuse. But the practical fulfillment of human rights is humanity for the oppressed. The practical realization of freedom is the liberation of the enslaved. The practical function of this Universal Declaration of Human Rights therefore can only be revolutionary.

In what respect should the Declaration of Human Rights be supplemented if it should have, not an idealistic, but a revolutionary significance? The ideal rights of man can certainly be extended. For example, the present definitions of the right to the freedom of religion are deficient. In my opinion, however, it would be more important to extend human rights with reference to social obligations. For me, the decisive issue is the transformation of rights which secure the freedom of individuals into obligations to liberate those whose rights are withheld by others. If the Universal Declaration of Human Rights is not to be only an ideal suspended above an inhuman world, but desires the realization of these rights, then rights must be articulated in terms of their realization. Up to the present time there is nothing expressed in the Universal Declaration about suffering within the world which is necessarily entailed in the struggle for liberation.

What theological links between the Christian faith and the tradition of human rights are capable of bearing weight and are fruitful?

These connecting concepts emerge historically in the process of humanization and Christianization of the world and have a historically shaped and delineated form. They stand between concrete

Christian practice and universal humanity as political and legal forms of life.

The theological tradition has perennially connected Christian practice and universal humanity by means of a Christian *doctrine of natural law* and a Christian doctrine of *creation*. This connection is only a theoretical one. The existing right of man is explained as a reflection of the right of God. By this means it is both recognized and maintained. A Christian doctrine of natural law really has nothing to add to the natural law. Rather in every case it has to free it from misuse.

For this study I would like to propose another way. In order to sketch that theory which grounds this event of liberation and makes it universally binding and which does this by defining man in terms of the freedom of his similitude to God, should we not begin from the concrete practice of the liberation of the unfree man through faith, love, and hope? Should we not begin with the practice of liberation in order then to outline that theory which combines this historical event with hope in the human kingdom of the new man and makes it accessible for every human being?

In the Old Testament, theological thought begins with Yahweh's liberation-history with Israel in the exodus and only afterward, and on this basis, comes to the confession that this God of liberation is the Creator of all things and the Redeemer of all people. In the New Testament, too, theological thought begins with the confession of Christ as the liberator and only then, and on this basis, comes to the doctrine of creation and to eschatology.

Translating this into a *theology of human rights* would likewise mean beginning with the *concrete theology of liberation* and, on this basis, presenting the universal meaning of this freedom as universal human right and the common future of this freedom as new humanity.

I think that only with this concrete starting point in the theology of liberation can universal theories and declarations about the freedom of man be protected from their misuse.

Thus I conceive the theological process of such a grounding in three steps:

(1) *Christian theology is theology of liberation, for it understands Christ in the comprehensive sense as liberator.*

(2) *The theology of liberation is the theology of man, for every man is defined by his similitude to God.*

(3) *The theology of liberation is the theology of the future, for the kingdom of the Son of man is the human future of man.*

Questions posed to step 1:

How does the Bible look if we read it with the eyes of the poor, the hungry, the outcasts, and the oppressed? Do we not assume a false standpoint over against the Bible when we read it as a book of religion or as a book of law or as a book of dogmatic ideologies, while failing to stand in solidarity with the oppressed?

The sick, the possessed, the leprous, the humiliated, and the godless experienced Jesus as a concrete liberator from their concrete misery and they believed in this liberation. From what is Christianity seeking to liberate men in the discipleship of Jesus, in its proclamation, its community, and its deeds? Do we understand faith as a concrete event of liberation or do we believe only in a freedom which does not really exist? Do we understand Jesus, in the comprehensive sense, as liberator from every unfreedom and inhumanity, or do we consider him only a religious liberator?

Jesus is experienced as liberator by those who are bound, by the oppressed and the guilt-laden, and their community with him is concrete freedom from their chains, their oppressions, and their guilt. But he was crucified by the powers and the principalities of the world according to their law. If they do not persecute Christianity today, they nevertheless would like to take the dangerous power of liberation away from it. How then is Christ conceived? As Lord of heaven, a new lawgiver, an unpolitical religious founder, or a guardian of order?

On which side does the church stand in one's own country? Has it become the political religion of the powerful in order to receive their goodwill and money? In each of our several countries, where and how does liberation for the oppressed proceed from ecclesiastical institutions and Christian actions?

Questions posed to step 2:

If a theology of liberation is a theology of man, because every man is defined by the image of God, then church and Christian practice can be realized not only in church and Christian circles, but must make the questions of man its own question. Yet how can the Christian caste-spirit and the mistrust of others be overcome?

For whom is the question of man the most important? For the inhuman, the dehumanized. Consequently, a church which makes the question of man its own question cannot simply "exist for all men"; it must exist for those robbed of human rights and freedoms. How can the church become the community of the poor and the oppressed and dissolve its ties with others who make them poor and oppress them?

What means can Christianity use for the liberation of man to freedom? Missionary means or also humanitarian measures? When is the use of revolutionary force necessary for the liberation of the oppressed? Can it be that, on the basis of existing declarations of human rights in particular countries, institutionalized tyranny is manifested? For example (a) politically through the rule of military cliques, (b) racially through the predominance of a white minority, (c) socially through the predominance of an exploiting class?

If an obvious tyranny has no right to power, is revolutionary power then justified?

Who is justified in and obligated to resistance? Is there a right of the people to revolution, as earlier in the church there was a right of the congregation to reformation?

In such situations can the political responsibility of individual Christians be distinguished from the commission of the church?

Questions posed to step 3:

Which ideal of the future is depicted in the Universal Declaration of Human Rights? Can it be combined with the hope in the "human kingdom of the Son of man," which, according to Daniel 7, is to cut off the kingdoms of the world?

To what degree does the Christian hope in the kingdom of God support and to what extent does it criticize the hope in the coming society of humanity, which is expressed in human rights?

How can there develop out of the ideal of human rights a concrete utopia which relates the intended human future of man to the specific political, social, and racial injustice of the present in order to overcome opposition and resistance?

By whom is this future of man represented today? By the public? How can the conscience of the world public be sharpened? By Christianity? How can the *oekumene* speak representatively for Christians who in certain countries cannot speak publicly? Does this damage the difficult position of those Christians or does it assist the struggle for liberation? Does the ecumenical bond of the churches give individual churches and Christians more independence over against the coercion of their own nation and social order? Does the struggle for the realization of human rights not presuppose an inner break in the national egoism and the class intellect or the racial mind-set? If Christians find their identity in the crucified Christ, then what relevance can national, cultural, and economic identity still have for them?

XII.

The Humanity of Living and Dying

I. MEDICINE FOR HUMANITY

It was Alexander Mitscherlich who in another context coined the harsh phrase, "medicine without humanity." We are taking it up here not as an accusation but as an indication of a problem.

In archaic times medicine was a part of religion. The medicine man was a priest and vice versa because the whole of life was interpreted by religious symbols and regulated by magical and ritual practices. To be sure, medicine in this situation was not particularly human; neither was religion. But the sick and their sicknesses were comprehended by the total religious conception of society. The triumphant advance of modern medicine stems from the use of the *methods* of the *natural sciences* and of recent technology. The transition from religion to natural science and technology has made medicine a science. The physician understands himself as a practicing natural scientist.

But this has its price: the totality of life in the variety of its other dimensions falls out of view. Cultural history, anthropology, sociology, and religion seldom occupy a central place in the course of medical education. Thus there arises the threat that what one might call the *personal dimension* of the sick person will be overlooked, that sickness will become an objective defect to be eliminated through repair. Only if everything subjective is excluded can we get a clear picture of the bodily priorities. Just as with all exact natural sciences, medicine as a natural science functions by means of the isolating of its object, its abstraction from other frameworks, the screening out of other problems and therefore its objectification. Since it has been possible to isolate the illness from the patient in theory and to grasp the entire chain of cause and effect from the agent to all important factors in the disease process it has been possible to determine a therapy with specific objective

Isolating is the key word here. First the sick person is isolated from the environment in which he lives and is brought into a hospital, in the more severe cases, to an isolated intensive care unit. Then the sickness is isolated from the person, that is, the sick person is reduced to a specific syndrome. If the typical paradigm symptoms of a sickness are analyzed in "a case" of this sickness, as the sick person is now called, then a therapy with specific objectives can be initiated. This process is as necessary as it is self-evident.

But it has become possible only through a long, tedious history in the self-understanding of man and it has its price. We can briefly recall the history. It begins with the West's dualistic image of man according to which an immortal soul dwells in a fragile, mortal body, as in a house, a ship, or a prison. This dualism provides a distance—a distance of the human self from his or her body. The body (*Körper*) is something which one has for a time, from birth to death. To be sure one *has* it closer, under the clothes so to speak, than any other possession. But it is also a possession which is at one's disposal and to be dominated.

This isolating of the bodily (*leiblichen*) existence from the body (*Körper*) which one has, this dualism of soul and body, became the foundation of the scientific and technical age, and it has persisted. For Descartes and his concept of the reflecting *I*, one's own body fell into the sphere of the objectively knowable and controllable *res extensae*; only the pineal gland connected it with the *res cogitans*. La Mettrie understood the body as a machine according to the paradigm of the most advanced technique of his time: the clock. We have come a long way beyond that. We understand the body as an *information- and systems-theory cycle of self-adjustment* (Bertalanffy). But with this we have not really gone beyond the fundamental isolating of the body from the center of life we call *soul* or *I* or *consciousness*. Rather we have simply succeeded in further isolating the body from the living of its life and in isolating sicknesses from the "open system" of the body.

I am exaggerating somewhat, but one can say in principle that in clinics the physiological and pathological functions are converted into a *data flow* through which one seeks to grasp specific extremities and aberrations. The subjectivity of the sick person

remains excluded. A symptom of this is the progressive abandonment of language between patient and physician. It is replaced by
the read-out of the instruments. The patient is no longer a direct
phenomenon but only represented by symbols which are bounded
by definite diagnostic limits and which permit only a quantitative
notion of the patient's individuality.

Human language becomes superfluous. In its extreme this fact
means: "The clinic is essentially mute" (P. Lüth). The clinic does
not speak with the patient, but bypasses him, and if it speaks at all
after his treatment and release, it addresses itself to the referring
physician. The patient becomes the object of data processing and
treatment. The patient must first adjust himself to becoming the
mute patient who is being treated by the clinic. Even this is not
always a simple process, for ultimately he is a human being and
not a thing. The patient must also personally come to terms with
his suffering and for this he would like to be taken seriously as a
subject with anxieties and sufferings. But which physician has time
for this or can take the time? If he can achieve it, he will be a
physician for fewer people. If he is a physician for many people,
then he cannot manage it.

If we are asking for a humane medicine which wants to serve
the humanity of persons and not just the proficiency of their physical functioning, we must indeed pursue the reverse course. That
is, after following the long way of *isolating* the sick person from
his or her life space, of isolating the body of the person, and of
isolating the sicknesses from the bodily system, we must also begin
the long march of *integration*.

Let us begin with the experience of man in his bodiliness. The
self-consciousness of man points to the fact that he can say "I" and
thereby mean himself. In English, one says "I am some*body*" and
in this way identifies himself *bodily*. In his experienced life, bodily
and spiritual functions harmonize in the unity of his person. He
exists bodily in spontaneous impression and spontaneous expression. In reflection he can simultaneously gain distance from himself and can recognize the bodiliness (*Leiblichkeit*) which he is as
the body (*Körper*) which he has. Recent philosophical anthropology (Helmut Plessner) has characterized this as the excentric
position of man. He *is* bodily and simultaneously *has* this body

(*Leib*) as his body (*Körper*). He lives in the double role of being and having and must again and again effect a balance of both roles. In this harmonious balance the spontaneous bodily existence has indeed the primary status and the experience of having, the secondary status.

Upon first awakening in the morning one says to oneself: "I am sick. I don't feel well." Only the fully wakened reflection localizes the pain so that one then says: "I have a stomach ache."

The history of Western anthropology shows how difficult was the development of the freedom of the soul, or the mind, or the I, over against the bodiliness of the body which one has. All dualistic theories of man were concerned to widen this *distance*. This was ethically necessary, since man had to struggle to free himself from drives and sufferings. This could be accomplished only through distance from and renunciation of everything connected with bodily existence. The ideal was the Stoic way of mortifying one's body and no longer being affected by any emotions. The ideal could also be the modern researcher who experiments on his own body and records his reactions with complete detachment.

As necessary as this process is for the independence of man, we are nevertheless experiencing today the consequences of its one-sidedness. We become aware of the repressed body only if it refuses to serve us. It is no longer recognized as a medium of the affective experience of the whole person: the *pathic* has been debased to the pathological. *Apathy*, which was so highly esteemed by earlier anthropology and ethics, is changed into indifference toward one's own as well as another's suffering. It is transformed into a coldness of feeling for everything living. The world which we dominate and use has nothing more to say to us.

If classical ethics was a theory of action, in the counter move there would be an *ethic of receptivity* in its place. In the midst of all struggle against inhuman and ruinous suffering and experience of pain, there also has to be developed a concept of meaningful human passion and an acceptance of meaningful human conflicts and suffering. An *ethic of the pathic*, without destroying the independence of the person, must teach people to allow themselves to be vulnerable, to allow themselves to be affected, and to develop their own spontaneity.

Such an ethic of the pathic, however, presupposes a new anthropology which allows all insights and therapies of the *body-having* (*Körper-Habens*) to be integrated together with this body in the *body-being* (*Leib-Sein*) of the person. The *category of having* has stifled the *category of human being*, not only economically and socially, but also medically. And if the category of being cannot catch up with the category of having, if the person can no longer integrate the analyzed and repaired body, there will emerge a whole social system of isolated function-bearers devoid of humanity. *Objectification* and *subjectification* belong together. The difficult process of regarding the body medically as the object-body and the sick person as the bearer of a type of sickness should be complemented by the no less tedious process of relating the object-body to the subject-body of the person and of integrating the sickness with the healing process through the person. Ludolf von Krehl once said: "There are no sicknesses as such. We know only sick people." That may sound polemical and one-sided, but in face of the medicine which treats "syndromes" of sickness and "cases" of sickness, it is important to remember the sick person and to ask about his sick or healthy humanity. The question whether the medicine which reduces itself to measurable data and diagnostic measures in relation to the "open system" of the object-body really wants to know something about man extends far beyond medicine to our social system: Does man want to know something about man? And how much time can we take for man himself in view of the immoderate claims made on us all by our social functions and roles?

Moving from *isolation* to *integration* therefore depends on integrating the *ordering of the body* into the *ordering of the whole person* and in again recognizing the sick person behind the sickness. It means also being able to accept oneself as a sick person in the sickness. The consequence would be that the patient could not appear merely in the role of a mute object of the physician's professional functions; rather the subjectivity of this object would again have to be expressed. The patient cannot merely provide feedback signals about himself in the clinical procedure. To be sure, in practice this is unavoidable, but it still does not educe his humanity. Once again, Ludolf von Krehl: "Man has the capacity to shape the process of his sickness through his bodily, his spiritual, or, expressed best, his human influence on precisely this process: The sick person is not only an object but always simultaneously a subject." How can the patient be taken into coresponsibility and enter into the process of healing as a *mature responsible partner*? What does he know of his sickness? Is it worth listening to him or is it better that he simply follow the physician's orders? The "demystification of objectivism" through the "introduction of the subject" (V. von Weizäcker) into pathology would teach us to understand sickness as something in which the *question of life's meaning* is kindled and in which experienced meaning or meaninglessness shows itself. The meaning of life, after all, is not health. Health is to be found in the service of this meaning which must be authenticated in sickness and in death. Can the physician enter into this human side of the sick person?

Many claim that the problems stem from the unfortunate but necessary specialization of medicine. In earlier times the house physician kept in view (1) the whole sick person, and (2) the sick person in the life surroundings of his home. It is certainly false to idealize the pretechnological house physician, for there never existed such a physician for every sick person. But it seems to me correct to hold to this memory of the house physician in (1) its reference to the *sick person* and (2) its reference to the *ecological consideration* of the patient in his own environment. The question is, how to eliminate the isolating of sickness from the sick person and the isolating of the sick person from his environment without also giving up a single method of precise scientific medicine? Would not an ecological integration of medicine, clinics, and patients be beneficial to all three? This would mean for medicine as science that it would have to extend itself toward sociology, psychology and—in the broadest sense of the word—care of souls (*Seelsorge*), that is, concern for the human being in his or her entirety. It would have to seek concrete connections to these other sciences of man. Medicine would then be not only a practical natural science but also a practical science of the humanities. For the practicing physician this would mean a conscious acceptance and development of the role of his office as a social agency for the crises and tensions of his patients—a role for social and spiritual as well as bodily help. Yet the office accumulates an expensive apparatus of diagnosis and therapy which can be amortized only through intensive use. In view of this apparatus, conversation with the patient, by virtue of which this room is called *Sprechzimmer* in German, becomes a time-robbing detriment.

What then is "health"? Does not the definition of health always employ social, cultural, and religious criteria? But are contemporary society's criteria "healthy" in a human sense, that is, humanly meaningful? Freud and many others have defined health as *capacity for work and pleasure*. If one is again capable of work and pleasure, one can be released as healed. This criterion corresponds exactly to a society which is built on production and consumption. Earlier and different societies have had quite different conceptions of health. The definition of the World Health Organization refers to health as a "condition of general well-being." But are the people capable of work and pleasure in our society generally and altogether "well"?

A medical healing does not have to agree with this society's standard of health in regard to its concern for the humanness of persons. Rather, in consideration of social suffering and the suffering of many at the hands of society, it can call such a standard of health into question. Medical therapy as part of the total therapy of the sick person does not need to become the servant and purveyor of the contemporary standards of society, when indeed these standards cannot really be called "human" and "healthy." "Medicine for the humanity of persons" can also acquire socially critical functions. The humanization of the socialized and accommodated person is a tremendous task, which such a medicine cannot, however, accomplish alone.

II. ON THE BEGINNING OF LIFE AND THE ORIGIN OF THE HUMANITY OF LIFE

I would like to relate the dimension of the humanity of life to the dimension of the vitality of life in two steps by asking about (1) the beginning and the origin of human life, and (2) the end and the death of human life. In both I would like to inquire about the quality of human life.

When does life begin? There has been a long-standing assumption that in dealing with this question one will also give a satisfactory scientific answer to the question about the essence of human life. In the contemporary precarious discussion of abortion this question becomes crucially important for legislators as well as for ethicists. I am not interested in entering here into this discussion, which already fills countless volumes. In relation to this question, I would merely like to clarify the two dimensions of which I spoke.

The more one engages in scientific research on the *beginning of life,* or, as it is often called, the beginning of a nascent life, the more difficult it becomes to describe the limits and to determine the exact date. There are too many intermediate links and transitional stages. Thus we must ask first, for what purpose is the beginning point to be ascertained? There seems to be one perspective in which the gynecologist speaks of a gestation period *post menstrationem* and *post conceptionem* or *post ovulationem* in order to arrive at the date of birth. There is another perspective in which the lawyer who practices forensic medicine asks about it in order to determine a paternity or to establish the criminality of an illegal abortion. From a scientific perspective the beginning of life results from a series of specific processes. Between fertilization and implantation a full seven days can be reckoned and only after several days subsequent to implantation can one really speak of a pregnancy. The "nascent life" is therefore accorded a different value, depending on whether one is considering the present *condition of the fetus* or the potential *future of the person.* Whoever, for whatever reason, advocates impunity for the practice of abortion is predisposed to concede *life* but not *human* life to the fetus of the first trimester. Conversely, whoever, again for whatever reason, is against abortion will see already in the three-month-old embryo the beginning of a future person.

In the context of the question of the admissibility or inadmissibility of an abortion the other dimension of human life always enters into the purely scientific establishment of the complicated processes which lead to the life of a person. This question can thus no longer be answered by means of the natural sciences. It is a question of value. The question of the *origin* of the humanness of life cannot be answered by a dating of the *beginning* of life in its protoforms.

In a position paper, written with three other Tübingen professors of theology, we have therefore made a distinction between protection against the destruction of *vitality* and protection against the destruction of *humanity*. Man is inexorably dependent upon both. His humanity is not less a constitutive element of human life (*menschlichen Lebens*) than is his vitality a constitutive element of humane life (*Menschen-Lebens*). A protection of the not-yet-born human life would be in itself a contradiction if it were not also protecting the humanity of the nascent life.

But where does the origin of this humanity lie if it is not identical with the biological beginning of life, however this may be dated? We began with the assumption that before the fertilization, during the pregnancy, and after the birth, it belongs to the essence of humane life (*Menschen-Lebens*) that it is *accepted* and *affirmed*, *recognized* and *loved*. Nascent humane life gains and develops its humanity only in the atmosphere and in the space of acceptance and recognition by others. *Acceptance* belongs to humane life as a necessity of life, particularly the life of a child, and is as important as nourishment and circulation of the blood. Life which is not accepted becomes spiritually and physically sick and dies. To the procreation, conception, and birth of a child there belongs constitutively the acceptance of the child by the parents and society. This is the human dimension of the biological process. One could therefore say: In the moment when the mother, the parents, the family—to name only those most proximately concerned—develop a relationship of acceptance and affirmation for the embryo, the atmosphere of humanity is established in which this nascent life can become a humane life.

If we accept this basic category of humanity, it follows that an *abortion* is to be viewed not as the first or the exclusive culpable denial of humanity. Rather, the *rejection* of a person's becoming and beyond that, the rejection of each person, is already such a denial of humanity. This extends, of course, far beyond individual persons. The construction of cities which are inimical to children then amounts to an impediment of acceptance and humanity.

On the other hand, this category allows for conscientiously weighing each individual case. There are always at least two people involved in acceptance. The acceptance of another presupposes inner identity and strength on the side of the accepting one. Without such requirements for acceptance of a nascent life, and thus a pregnancy, self-dissolution and self-destruction set in to a point where one can no longer speak of acceptance and love.

A merely biological argumentation does not suffice. Is the quality of life to be conferred on the embryo or the quality of *human* life? Conversely, an exclusively personal argumentation is also inadequate, since the human nonrecognition and refusal of nascent life can be revoked. A child, who was at first rejected as nascent life, may later be so intensely loved by parents that they no longer want to be without the child; an abortion, however, is irreversible. If it is now the case that, in this question, medical, social, personal, and moral dimensions are entangled, then counseling in individual cases and deliberation over legislation and social conditions must take place in an atmosphere of collective action by various persons and agencies.

III. ON THE END OF THE BODY AND THE DEATH OF MAN

The relationships at the end and death of man's life are similar, I believe, to those at the beginning and origin of human life. If at the beginning it is a question of the human *acceptance* of life, here it is a question of the human *surrendering of life*. And again we stand before the question of how the medically ascertainable *exitus* is related to the *death of man*.

Everyone knows that human life is mortal, but when and how dying happens today is something that only a very few know. Everyone knows that everywhere and in every moment people are dying, but the more durable, the more conscious attitude toward death is lacking. In former times the direct experience of the death of others was a part of the total experience of life. Children experienced the sicknesses and death of the aged in the family. They spoke with the dying person, saw the corpse, and experienced the mourning. Today this has changed. The mortality of children has receded and the life expectancy has risen twofold. The seriously ill disappear from active life into the hospital. The aged live more and more among their own kind in homes for the aged. The burial with the accompanying rituals is delegated to the mortuary. With this the experience of death vanishes from the center of society.

The consciousness of death is separated from active life. With the isolating of the seriously ill and aged—that is, those who are nearest to death—the direct contact with death is lost to society. And before *physical death* reaches them, many aged and sick people already suffer a *social death,* because no one any longer takes notice of them and relationships to them are broken off. The retired man whose decaying corpse was found in his Berlin apartment four weeks after his death is one symptom of this. Only the violent traffic death on the streets is experienced by our children, and even then only momentarily, without the development of any disposition toward it and almost with no inward working-through of the experience. For the public such a death is a regrettable incident. For the drivers it is only a traffic disturbance until finally the victim is transported off with red flashing lights and the traffic again flows "smoothly."

What kind of mourning can really still be experienced publicly? "The mourner no longer has any status" (Bally). But if the contact with death, if the contact with the dying, if mourning in which the experience of death is inwardly worked through, if these are repressed, are we not then in the midst of a tremendous *repression?* And if this is so, then the consequence of such a repression is assuredly a growing *apathy* and a continually deepening *inability to love.*

Medical work turns its efforts against the premature, un-"natural" death and toward the prolongation of life. That is as it should be for the professional practice of medicine. A similar repression of dying and all conscious human attitudes toward death should not, however, be an unconscious result of this. When in the presence of the dying the medical art has come to an end, the human being in the physician is after all still "on call." One must therefore lament the fact that in many hospitals death still occurs in the corridor, in the laundry, or in equipment stations. This takes from the dying one his dignity as a person; he is then regarded as only a hopeless case. One must as well lament the fact that people delegate the right to their own death to "death at the hand of the physician" (Rilke). In the environs of medico-technical efforts, moreover, death is frequently represented as a mishap, a technical error, or merely the patient's *exitus,* from whose approach the physician vanishes in order to attend to other sick people because he can do nothing more. Dying is then no longer a *human process* in which other human beings are present as human beings.

In this connection the question of whether and how the physician, if he is certain, should tell the dying person the truth, has often been discussed. If one theoretically answers in the negative and in practice avoids it, then this is, as recent investigations show, not so much an act of consideration but more often an expression of the embarrassment on the part of physicians and nurses. More than sixty percent of the dying obviously know what their condition is and wait for a language that will reach them. Only a few, however, have learned this language.

Death can be ascertained medically in the dying away of vital organs. Currently the irreversible death of the brain is viewed as the concrete symbol for the death of man. After this there is no longer a duty to "maintain life," that is, the further functioning of other organs. In the sense of the maintenance of *life,* insofar as it is a question of *human* life, there is also evidently no obligation to bring back into life a dying person day by day so that he has again to suffer through dying from night to night if there is no substantial prospect for life.

The death of man—that is, the death of the person—is of course tied to the death of the body, but it has other, namely, human dimensions. In the Middle Ages there was an extensive literature about the *Ars moriendi.* Luther wrote a gripping "Sermon on the Preparation for Death." Today such books are extremely rare. Yet is dying an art which we can learn? Obviously it is not an art which we can learn through repetition, but it is an art which we can learn through attitudes toward life, suffering, and dying and through love and mourning.

What is at stake in the *Ars moriendi?* It is concerned with the human act of *surrendering* life, or the affirmation of dying, and of the acceptance of death. Just as a person in *love* goes outside of himself, affirms another despite the other's unacceptability and thus becomes vulnerable, so affirmed dying is an act of loving surrender. Just as *faith* means giving daily out of one's own anxious and covetous hand and trusting the one who gives life, so affirmed

dying means to give oneself finally out of one's own hands and to
trust the one who takes the life which he gave. *Acceptance* and
surrender are the two basic acts which constitute the humanity of
life. One can *surrender* oneself to the extent that one has experienced acceptance, and one can accept oneself to the extent that
one has experienced surrender. Other people are necessary for
these basic acts. But in this encounter with other people also
belongs the mystery of the greater love out of which come life,
death, and likewise the power of accepting and surrendering life.
This divine love makes life vital here and now and at the same
time makes death deadly. This love of God also makes life meaningful here and now in surrender, in the acceptance of human
wounds, and finally in the acceptance of death. The medical possibilities which are pushing back the limits of life and death will
be used in a human way only if human beings experience life
more humanly and consciously and prepare themselves through
love in life for surrender in death. The mere prolongation of life
does not yet contain this human meaning, just as the mere conception and birth of human life do not bring forth human life as
human.

IV. SUMMARY

Having spoken of the humanity and the meaning of human life
in reference to the origin and the death of human life, we can
now make a brief summary.

The meaning of human life is not mere life or survival; rather
biological life stands in service of humaneness.

Health and ability to function are not the meaning of human
life; rather health and the ability to function physically and
spiritually stand in service to this meaning.

This meaning—namely, to fill life with humanity, with acceptance and surrender, with interest and love—is therefore authenticated also in sicknesses and in dying by the sick and dying person.

The medical struggle against sickness and premature death must
not lead to repression of the awareness of human suffering or of
the human art of dying and mourning.

Medicine can most certainly free itself from technocratic thinking which does everything it can without asking about its meaning for the humanity of man.

After having achieved specialization, we need a comprehensive conception of *human illness* in its bodily, spiritual, social, and transcendental dimensions.

For this we need a comprehensive understanding of *health* in the sense of a meaningful humanity.

And finally, with all this we need a cooperation of the various therapies in the medical, social, and human sphere with a view toward what deserves to be called, in an ultimate, all-encompassing, and unqualified sense, salvation—*soteria*—*shalom*. What we know of salvation in this life comes only through faith and hope.

XIII.

Bringing Peace to a Divided World

I

Everyone today is talking about peace, and the churches most of all. "Peace be with you" is the liturgical greeting, and "Grant us peace" is the church's petition. Sunday after Sunday, year after year, century after century, the gospel of God and the yearnings of mankind are summarized in one word—peace!

Everyone, including ourselves, may be talking about peace, but the word does not mean the same thing to everyone. *What* do we mean by "peace"? *Whose* peace are we proclaiming? *Who* is to benefit from it?

"Leave me in peace," say some, and we know that they want to be let alone. "Have peace in your heart," say others, meaning "Ignore the rest of the world." "Peace to all men of good will"— but not to the others, whose will is opposed to ours. "Peace to the cottages, war to the palaces!" shouted the troops of the French Revolution. "Peace will come only after capitalism is abolished," say the revolutionaries of today. And their opponents reply, "The only way to negotiate with Communists is to hold a gun over them." Peace is having such a hard time these days because everybody has his own peace in mind.

When Christians speak of peace, they often mean only the peace "which passes all understanding" (Phil. 4:7), and forget the "peace on earth" of the Christmas story (Lk. 2:14). It is true that the "gospel of peace" (Eph. 6:15) creates the *hope of faith,* but nowadays we must learn how to put this *hope into action* on earth. We have to stop using the traditional abstract language of God's peace, language which does nothing for anyone, and speak concretely of peace while doing something to overcome poverty, violence, and the destruction of life. To put hope into action, we must interpret the gospel of peace politically.

By a political interpretation I mean words that have to do with experience and action. In a broader sense, I mean the transition from a pure theory to a practical one. Today we need a social and political interpretation of the great and weighty words we all learned in church—words like "sin," "death," and "the devil" on the one hand and "forgiveness," "resurrection," and "redemption" on the other. For with our abstract and religious language we have indeed passed on the gospel of peace, but at the same time we have rendered it ineffective.

It is one thing to acquire a theological notion of *what* constitutes the church of God's peace in the truth of Christ, but it is something else to recognize practically *where* and *how* the church arrives at the truth of Christ. It is irresponsible of Christians to hope for God's peace unless they go where men are at war and hoist the flag of peace between the lines of those who are about to kill each other. Anything else would be mere religious self-gratification, contempt for Christ who was crucified right in the middle of this world.

II

Working for peace is not what it used to be. In the age of science and technology, world peace has become the absolutely necessary condition for the survival of the human race. War is no longer a possible alternative to peace. The one alternative to world peace is world annihilation, whether by atomic suicide, the escalation of social injustice, or the creeping ecological death of industrial societies. The future is no longer open as it was in former times, when, after plagues and war, nature could repair the damage unassisted. Either we make a future for ourselves, our children, and mankind, or we drop the future into the lap of death. "One world or none"—the alternative is as simple as that.

In former times, "history" was in the plural. Each nation and each religion had its own history—its own past and its own future. World history did not exist, only histories of men in the world. Today we are inescapably entering one world common to all; consequently history is undergoing a radical transformation, we shall continue to have pasts and traditions in the plural, but we shall have a future and a hope only in the singular. This means that the future can no longer be the continuation of our national, cultural, and religious pasts; it must be something new. On this threshold of history, the alternative is simple: united we stand, divided we fall.

The new community of mankind must recognize that world peace is the condition for survival and must bring it about. What shape will this community take? Who will be responsible for peace? The more control man gets over nature and destiny, the more responsibility is laid on him. Today man's destiny is more than ever a political destiny, but this has not yet made politics more human.

The military, economic, and technological power of certain nations is growing enormously, but the political and juridical agencies responsible for the use of this power have not kept up with this growth; instead they remain restricted to certain nations and classes. The military and economic power of the U.S., the U.S.S.R., and the Common Market exercises a controlling influence over all human beings and all life on earth. This power is concentrated in the hands of a few. Thus the power of technology has become universal, while responsibility remains provincial. This imbalance endangers world peace; it is the reason we do not have world peace now, because most decisions are still made in one's own national, racial, or class self-interest.

The only way responsible control can be exercised over universal military and economic power is through world government. Divided mankind must organize itself if it wants world peace. But world government does not exist. The idea seems quite realistic when we consider the deadly threat to mankind, but utopian when we consider the political situation. Therefore we must devise transitional forms. If world peace can be achieved only through world government, then particular governments and agencies have a right to exist only if they contribute to world peace and help bring about world government.

This holds not only for individual nations but also for economic organizations and religions and churches. National foreign policy should be transformed into world domestic policy. In every decision, the crucial question must be, not "how does it help my people?" but "how does it promote the general peace?" Church policy regarding other churches must likewise be transformed into the ecumenical domestic policy of the one Church of Christ. *Solidarity* in combating the threat of death facing everyone must have priority over *loyalty*: every selfish self-interest on the part of nations, classes, and religions is today an obstacle to peace. In learning the new way of thinking, we have a long road to travel and a short time to do it in. Anyone who tries to think this way will find himself accused of "fouling his own nest," of treason to his country or his class. The truth is, however, that he is a child of liberty and an heir of the future.

How then shall we define peace? Our history is so full of sad experiences that our definitions tend to be negative more often than positive. Johan Galtung defines peace as "a way of living without violence or threat of violence, without oppression or aggression." That is why in conflicts we find it easier to agree to a cease-fire, a non-interference pact, or a non-aggression treaty, than to a real peace treaty, and this is true of the church as well. This negative description of peace is important but it does not go far enough. It must be filled out with a positive vision; otherwise the matter for conflict is not cleared away and the weapons are, as they say of warships, just put in mothballs.

Another definition of peace, then, might be the integration of contending parties into a larger system which satisfies the demands of social justice. But even this vision is a description of the way to peace rather than the peace at which we wish to arrive. The constitution of ultimate peace can only be known through hope and faith.

While history endures, however, we need a provisional constitution of peace leading to the fulfillment for which we hope. The "gospel of peace" creates hope in faith, but hope in action, already in the war-torn present, is on the lookout for ways in which that transcendent peace can be realized in anticipation. "Provisional peace" is not an ideal but a real process. It allows fighting enemies to become quarreling partners. Deadly conflict is steered onto the path of non-lethal controversy. People begin to attend to the common defense against what menaces them all, while their unavoidable differences are localized and relativized. The people of Crete, history tells us, always fought among themselves, but against a common enemy they closed ranks. Today divided mankind sees its common enemy looming ever larger. It is universal suicide. To vanquish this danger, the quarreling parties must close ranks, limit their differences, and settle them without threatening to kill each other.

As long as we are still on the way to peace, we cannot abolish force altogether, but we can control and limit its use. As travelers toward peace, we are not yet in the kingdom of freedom, but we can experience concrete acts of liberation from economic and political oppression. As pilgrims to the city of peace, we have not yet found true happiness, but we can help root out the causes of mass misery.

The road to peace is a process in several dimensions simultaneously. It must break four vicious circles, namely, the circles of (1) poverty and exploitation, (2) violence and oppression, (3) racial and cultural alienation, and (4) destruction of nature through industrial progress. The road to peace leads right through these vicious circles. This is the concrete meaning of giving an "account of the hope that is in you" (1 Pet. 3:15) in the face of mankind's universal discouragement and desperation.

Today these vicious circles have devilish power; they interlock like links in a chain; and they lead to death. Peace work, therefore, must look for political, economic, cultural, and religious ways that lead to life. Hope in action must produce images and anticipations of peace that will make the hope of faith credible.

III

What can the churches do for peace? The churches not only talk about peace in heaven and on earth but each of them understands itself to be a witness to, a sign and anticipation of, the *shalom* which embraces God, man, and all of creation. But before a church talks about peace, it has already spoken through the way it actually lives, its organization within society at large, its policies and politics. The reality of the churches does not always bear witness to the peace they prattle so much about; it often contradicts it. Hence, before asking what the churches can do, we must ask, What are the conditions for the churches to make any contribution whatsoever to world peace? As I have said, agencies can prove their claims only by serving the future of man and world peace. Their right to exist must be based on their actions on behalf of the peace of the future *whole*. Every claim to absoluteness is an obstacle to this peace. Every refusal to cooperate is a threat to peace. This has consequences for Christendom as a whole.

The churches can proclaim the universality of God's love for all men in Christ no longer by means of their own claim to absoluteness but only in open-minded dialogue and unreserved cooperation with groups which believe differently. God's truth is universal and his love knows no bounds, but the church is not universal. It is not yet the kingdom of God and of peace, but at best a foretaste of it. The church can represent the peace of God only by being open to everyone.

The only people who refuse to dialogue with Jews, Buddhists, and Marxists are those who either are anxious about their own faith or wish to obliterate the truths of Israel, Buddhism, or Marxism. Participants in dialogue, however, do not lose their own identity, they make its outlines clearer. In dialogue the Christian faith is not relativized but brought into living relationships. The more a church takes to heart the solidarity of the Crucified One with all men, the more relevant it becomes for other men and the more recognizable is its Christian identity.

A claim to lordship on the part of the church would contradict the lordship of Christ, who came to serve and not to be served. His service was given first of all to sinners and publicans, the poor and outcast, the downtrodden and hopeless. Were the church to follow his example, it would necessarily become a liberating church for the poor, the oppressed, the alienated, and all whom our society puts in the shadow of death. By serving the oppressed first, Christianity in truth serves all men. For, without the liberation of the poor, blacks, women, the sick, the aged, and those without hope, the others cannot become truly human, and humanity cannot attain to any community that deserves to be called human.

It further follows that Christianity can no longer present itself to this divided world in separated churches, each denying the others' claims to truth and refusing them fellowship. Despite the continuing fragmentation of Christians into religious confessions and political parties, there have always been Christians who knew that the church is one in Christ. Today this knowledge is trying to incarnate itself in the ecumenical movement. Only an ecumenically unified Christianity can become the body of Christ's truth. Only ecumenical peace in the church bears visible witness to the gospel of peace. The ecumenical movement locally and worldwide is an image and an anticipation of the peace Christians hope for.

Resistance is never stronger, however, than in the area of religious feelings. We run up against denominational exclusiveness, a provincial mentality with regard to church structures, seemingly unbreakable ties to a particular national state or to a particular social order. Periodically, after the churches have drawn a bit closer to each other, many Christians seem to undergo an identity-crisis. They are afraid they will lose their distinctiveness, and so they pull back. Then their contact with the World Council of Churches fades away.

The path the ecumenical movement must follow seems to me clearly marked. It has already led from *anathema* to *dialogue*. From dialogue it led to *cooperation* in ecumenical discussion groups and in service work. From cooperation between separated churches it must now lead to the toleration and the settlement of differences within the one church. It must move from cooperation to *council*. Conciliar life is not life without conflict but life with differences—which are tolerated and eliminated. When this happens, the way will be open to church unity in doctrine, worship, and political action.

Finally it follows that the individual churches must, through the ecumenical process, free themselves from their ties to nation, tribe, race, and class. Many churches already find that belonging to a worldwide fellowship gives them support in the critical stance they take toward the societies in which they live. As social bodies, the churches, of course, cannot be entirely detached from the interests of the nation, race, or class in which they exist. But automatic compliance with the demands of the nation and desires of a particular class has often led to the glorification of war, the blessing of arms and society's idols. Nations and societies push the churches into the role of a "civil religion," whose job it is to justify hostility toward the enemies of the state and to sanction injustice in the country itself. This robs the church of its identity; for it can be itself only in the crucified Christ. It is essential, therefore, that with all necessary accommodation the churches acquire their proper critical freedom. Otherwise they cannot act on behalf of world peace. This liberation of the churches is much helped by their belonging to a supranational association of a nongovernmental kind, such as Roman Catholicism or the Geneva World Council.

On the other hand, all the large churches are faced with the problem of all large organizations: they must adapt themselves to the opinion of the majority of their members. For their liberation, therefore, they need innovation groups at the grass roots— groups which will be less cautious than the administrators and more thoroughgoing than the average member in following Christ by working for peace. Ever since the transformation of the ancient church into the state church, there have been radical groups of this kind which in the name of Christ refused to conform to society. Some were rejected as sectarians, fanatics, and heretics; others accepted in the form of monastic and lay orders. The Mennonites, Quakers, and Churches of the Brethren refused to bear arms. They used to be condemned by the large churches; nowadays they are recognized as the "historic peace churches."

In the future it will be necessary to reckon with a similar double form of Christianity—large churches and innovation groups. If the large churches are going to carry on any peace work, they must free themselves, with the help of the innovation groups, from political and social constraint. On the other side of the coin, innovation groups can be effective only if they influence large churches by their example. There are a lot of unofficial, grassroots ecumenical get-togethers nowadays—action groups, *shalom* groups, student groups, Christian communes, mixed-marriage groups, and eucharistic communities. The large churches should not write them off as irregular or marginal phenomena but accept them as pacesetters. The church needs them if it is to be free.

The Christian church cannot work effectively for peace in the world unless it (1) is open to dialogue, (2) stands up for the liberation of those in misery, (3) heals its own schisms in councils, (4) liberates itself from the pressure exercised by nations and the ruling classes, (5) attempts to follow the innovation groups on the path of radical discipleship and to learn from their experiments.

IV

The gospel of peace must be put into action in the vicious circles in which human beings are actually wasting away and in which the threat of universal death is quite real. These are cycles from which there is no release, in which even the best leads to more evil. They are processes with negative feedback, by means of which life-systems gradually bring about their own termination. For those who try to break such circles, the prayer "Deliver us from evil" has become political. And, as Erich Fromm says, where death-oriented systems can be reoriented to life, belief in the resurrection becomes realistic.

Class differences within particular societies as well as between the advanced industrial nations and the underdeveloped agrarian countries create the first vicious circle, that of *poverty*. The economic systems in which we work keep moving us forward at an unequal, unsynchronized, and unjust rate. Per capita income, it is true, is increasing on the average, but the increases are not being shared equally by all. For individuals and whole population segments are finding their poverty not eliminated but locked into a cycle of poverty, work, and exploitation. Millions of immigrant workers in northern Europe are caught in this hopeless circle. Likewise the nonindustrialized countries see the price of agricultural products on the world market falling while the price of industrial goods rises. These countries keep sinking deeper into debt and never emerge from poverty and dependence.

The popular West German news magazine *Der Spiegel* reported that "poverty, police, courts, and prisons" form a vicious circle "inside which black America fights for its freedom. It was in this ring that the nonviolent Martin Luther King was struck down. It is a hopeless circle." In a global view, we are all working in a circle which is making the rich nations ever richer and the poor nations ever poorer. From this circle there is emerging a world nutritional crisis which will spell starvation for millions.

For the poor and starving in this vicious circle, "God is not dead—he is bread." If, with Paul Tillich, we define God as ultimate concern, then for them his concrete presence takes the form of bread. They bear in their bodies the costs of the one-sided economic growth that benefits only a few. And their misery will have repercussions on the rich and what they stand for.

The only way out of this vicious circle is for all parties to work hard for social justice, for the redistribution of economic power. What is needed is not aid to developing countries but social justice. "Feed the starving" is necessary, but only during the transition to a more just world economic system. Christians are called on not only to show love but to have faith. In the poor, the starving, and the prisoners, they are to see the poor, starving, prisoner Christ, and in his least brethren they are to recognize themselves.

In the vicious circle of poverty lurks the *vicious circle of violence*. It too is found in particular societies as a result of dictatorship or the dominance of a single class. And it is found between powerful and weak nations. Violence generates counterviolence, dictatorship generates rebellion, oppression costs millions of lives. The circles become hopeless: oppression gets better organized after each unsuccessful uprising. Successful uprisings often lead to the organization of new oppression. The increase in organized force and unorganized counterforce bodes ill for all.

Many are the localities where poverty, despair, drugs, violent crime, prison, and so on form a pattern from which there is no exit. On the international level the armaments race is leading us into a similar dead-end street. Until now the military deterrent systems have insured peace, but today they are leading us into a phase of instability. The possibility of the great war is greater because mutual insecurity is growing. As the experts clearly predicted, the course of the armaments race is a perpetually open spiral downward into nothingness. Furthermore, new weapons systems are not paid for entirely within the economy of one nation, they are a drain on the world economy too. Military-industrial complexes arise which eat up precisely the material needed to build up the infrastructure—schools, health care, and protection of the environment. The emphasis on military security produces malignant tumors in our society and this is one of the chief reasons why it is a sick society.

Those who are oppressed and menaced by this vicious circle of violence experience the presence of God as liberation and hope. Here the concrete meaning of "working for God's peace" is getting human rights recognized. It means paying attention to the right to resist the dictatorship of individuals or whole classes and races. On the international level, it means the progressive dismantling of threatening military systems and the construction of confidence-producing political systems. Mutual inspection is necessary, to be sure, but it does not go far enough. No technology can control military armaments one hundred percent. And so we must arouse the powers of trust. Without it, controls do not work. Christians, in my opinion, have the task of working with the oppressed to reduce anxiety, hysteria, and violence, of achieving first economic and then political freedom, and finally of creating a climate of trust in the vicious circle of mistrust and fear. The large churches, in my opinion, have the task of paving the way for political peace agreements. They can often succeed at this because they are *nongovernmental international organizations*. And political settlements need such preparations.

Within the vicious circle of violence lurks that of *racial and cultural alienation*. Human beings are made pitiable and tame by robbing them of their identity and degrading them to the level of manipulable things. Then they lose their names and their self-confidence and are molded in the image of their masters. No people can overcome poverty and oppression without being liberated from cultural, colonialistic, and ideological alienation. Often poverty and violence are eliminated only at the cost of more alienation of this sort. Then people go on living in relative freedom, but without knowing who they really are.

In this context, peace means "allowing people to experience identity, self-confidence, and self-respect." Only when the other is respected in his otherness can one become fully oneself and display one's racial and cultural identity. In the vicious circle of alienation, the presence of God is experienced as identity achieved in and through the recognition of others. God is not dead. He is present in the new experience of identity and in the recognition of others.

This is not the place to develop a new anti-racism program. The conflict is often between integration and identity. I would think that respect for racial difference and the consciousness of racial identity go together. Integration is not supposed to make every-body alike. Identity cannot mean permanent separation. Self-respect and respect for the other belong together. This can be achieved if people of different races meet each other without fear, without arrogance, and without guilt-feelings.

In the vicious circles of poverty, violence, and alienation, we recognize today an even more encompassing deathly spiral—the *vicious circle of the destruction of nature.* Industrialization, in-spired by an unreflective faith in progress, has irreparably upset the balance of nature. "The limits of growth" (see Meadows's MIT study, 1972) can already be calculated. Unless we find a com-promise between progress and social equilibrium, ecological death is not only to be feared—it can be dated. The whole magnificent undertaking which was the industrial revolution is coming to an end in the ecological crisis. Up to this point no technological solu-tion has been found. We must radically alter the centuries-old creeds and value-systems that make us produce and consume more and more.

Yet few things are more stable than the value-systems which people take for granted, according to social psychology. A change in values is always very painful. With almost messianic yearning, our parents and grandparents invested all their hopes in work, mechanical equipment, profit, and progress. The results are dis-illusioning—in fact, destructive. Individual efforts to protect the environment and the efforts of individual nations are not going to hold the ecological crisis off any longer. It can be checked only if all forces are mobilized and internationally coordinated.

If the industrial giants were made to pay for the restoration of the environment which they have destroyed, their costs would probably outstrip their profits. The Ruhr valley has many aban-doned coal mines and coal processing facilities. The countryside looks like the aftermath of a bombing raid. Yet people live there. Who is going to pay for restoring their environment? Mine profits are paid to the owners. The burden now falls on the taxpayer. Faced with a similar destruction of the environment and the threat of self-destruction, British experts have demanded a change in the whole theory of society and economy.

For those threatened with ecological death, God is present and can be experienced in the joy of existing and the peace of creation. In this context peace means "eliminating the hubris that makes man the slaveholder and exploiter of nature, and building up an attitude of partnership with nature instead." Nature is not an object but a world of living beings with their own rights. The Western values of conquest and control of nature must give way to the ancient values of the joy of living and reverence for the creation. Life's worth does not lie in having and processing but in existing with others in the world God has made for us. To reorient our values from economy to ecology, we must stop calculating and augmenting the quantity of life and start appreciating the quality of life. Being is more than having, the joy of living is more than maximizing profits, peace is worth more than power.

Paul (Rom. 8:19–23) regards the creation as anxiously awaiting the appearance of the free sons of God. Today we should ask ourselves what hope creation can find in the actions of mankind. None, up till now. The "free sons of God" have been few and far between. I hazard the conjecture that, if we reorient our society's life-values, we will find a great deal of relevance in the old, meditative, doxological forms of faith and life practiced by the ancient church and the monks.

V

We have spoken of changes in the concrete presence of God in the four vicious circles of modern life. God is present as bread, as freedom, as identity, and as peace. Each of his concrete presences directs us to something further. By this I mean to describe the universal in the concrete, the transcendent in the categorical, the eschatological in the everyday occurrence.

This is sacramental language. It is concrete without being pragmatic, universal without being abstract. Its concepts are open: like symbols, they are not cut-and-dried statements of what is but invitations to rethink, to discover, and to adopt new modes of behavior. If there is anything theological in the process of the real liberations that are going on, it will show itself in this kind of linguistic iconoclasm, which smashes the fetishism of rigid concepts and the idolatry of the status quo.

Faced with the scientific predictions of doomsday, there are those who believe that man is in the process of transforming his world into a living hell. Many hearts are gripped by blind fear. The future looks dark. People don't know where to turn; they become demoralized, unable to organize their lives. Like a rabbit that sees a snake, they are paralyzed by their view of the future. Some take refuge in enjoying the present moment; their motto is "after us, the deluge." Others denounce in anger and disgust this whole rotten society. The abyss of Godforsakenness and hopelessness is experienced in various ways, but it is always this abyss which makes man experience the various spheres of suffering we mentioned as vicious circles from which there is no escape.

In this context, Christian peace work means bearing witness to the human God who, in giving himself up to death on the cross, has suffered through the hell of abandonment and thereby has opened up the future to all who are abandoned. Hell lies not before us but behind us. In his death on the cross, he has vanquished it for us. In the brotherhood of Christ, the abandoned are not abandoned but taken in and brought back to life.

In view of the anxiety of our age, "the word about the cross" must lead to "giving an account of the hope." We give this account when we exorcise demons and feelings of impending doom. When people are set free from irrational fear, from the paralysis of anxiety, from escaping into fantasies, from the militant urge to destroy, then they find the courage resolutely and patiently to do what is necessary to break the vicious circles we spoke of. The demoralized society surrenders to its own death wish; only rebirth to living hope brings back the wish to live—and this is true socially and politically as well as personally.

Without the hope of faith, there is no ground for hope in action. Without hope in action, there are no results from the hope of faith. Without a presence for peace in the vicious circles, giving an account of our hope remains abstract and of no help to anyone. Without the growth and spread of the hope of faith, however, all programs for peace and campaigns for liberation fall short of their marks, become pragmatic, and quickly succumb to weariness.

The time for peace is obviously short. May Christians wake up soon and, in this divided world, bear witness to the living peace.

XIV.

On Hope as an Experiment: A Postlude

The theme *hope and the future* appeared at the center of the philosophical, theological, and cultural discussions of the 1960s. Many thought that this theme would run its course and subside together with the aura of unrest and turmoil in those years. This has not been the case. A discovery and a new conception do not pass away with the times of the discovery and the conception. Living on as a discovery and a new insight, the theme of hope and the future forces us to come to terms with it in the midst of new experiences of history.

I

In this period *hope* became visible as that which makes human life vital. Whereas other living creatures are hopelessly sacrificed to a situation of no exit, man can set over against it a liberating power—hope. If the hope which is sustaining him dies, he also succumbs to an internal catastrophe. Philosophical reflection on the categories *future* and *possibility* create a new understanding of being as history. The key factor in medieval theology and sacramental life of the church was the supernatural *reality of love.* The Reformation shifted the focus to the *power of faith* and the congregation. When we come to the peculiar trends of modern times, we speak of secularization, emancipation, and enlightenment. But why did Kant believe that religion is supposed to answer the fundamental question, *What may I hope for?* In former epochs one did not approach religion with this question. The development of the theological doctrine of hope (eschatology) allowed us finally to take hold of the third dimension of Christianity. Only with the beginning of modern times did the *primacy of hope* seem to alternate with the primacy of faith and love. It was not explicitly the Christian hope which first appeared. Rather the modern primacy of hope appeared most distinctly in political messianism, the Enlightenment exodus from the constraint of tradition, and the enthusiasm of that spirit which no longer needed any mediation to God.

It became all the more urgent, then, after the rediscovery of biblical eschatology at the beginning of the twentieth century, to develop systematically a *theology of hope*. Grounded in the biblical promissory history and directed toward the promised kingdom, the Christian hope could then become responsible amid the revolutions and the repressions of the modern world. The recent theological reflection on this *responsible hope* works self-consciously out of three historical situations: firstly and immediately in the various movements of the sixties, secondly and more comprehensively in the modern history of freedom following the Reformation and medieval periods, and finally and most basically in the originating events of the Bible's promissory history which has called Judaism and Christianity into being and which must determine their life.

The theme *hope and the future* is therefore not a momentary theme or a passing fashion. It is the essential theme of Christian faith and of that love which in the modern context and today more than ever has to be worked out. The centrality of this theme comes into focus as one sees theology seizing on one fad after another. In order to indicate what the learning of hope means for Christianity, we can turn to Franz Rosenzweig:

If love was quite feminine, and faith very masculine, it is only hope that is ever childlike; in Christianity the commandment to "be as children" begins to be fulfilled only in it. . . . Faith and love, the old forces, are integrated into hope. From the child's sense of hope they derive new strength, so as to renew their youth "like the eagles."[1]

II

Hope is an experiment with God, with oneself, and with history. If one begins with experiences, one arrives with some degree of maturity at wisdom. But the proverbs which express the everyday wisdom of experience tend to emphasize resignation more than hope: "He who lives on hope dies of hunger." But if we look more closely at beginnings, we shall see that every beginning contains a surplus of hope. Otherwise one would begin nothing new but remain as one is and hold on to what one has. Whoever begins with hope is aiming to create new experiences. Hope does not guarantee that one will have only the wished-for experiences. Life in hope entails risk and leads one into danger and confirmation, disappointment and surprise. We must therefore speak of the *experiment of hope.*

An experiment tests out an object in order to bring it into the realm of experience. In the experiment of hope the object at stake is also always one's own life. The observer is himself the person experimented on, for it is the experiment of his life in which he is engaged. Ultimately each person can make such an experiment with his or her life only once. Hope must therefore be sufficiently comprehensive and profound. It must encompass happiness and pain, love and mourning, life and death if it is not to lead us into illusion. If one is searching for something new here, one is at the same time researching oneself. Hope liberates the experiment of life from prejudgments and securities and opens it up for the experience of living and dying. But it also has a tempting side, for it puts us to the test and leads us into danger. Therefore no one should enter into it frivolously, since no one can make an easy finish out of this experiment. Those who finish things too easily and all those who think that they are already finished shrink before this experiment. Are not such people subject to a greater danger—to miss completely their lives?

These two sides of the experiment—experience and temptation —emerge sharply in *Christian hope.* Those who enter into it lose everything that offers them security and reliance; their lives are placed in the life and the future appearance of the Son of man. In community with Jesus, the Son of man, they have new experiences, experiences of poverty and certainty, of certainty in poverty as well as poverty in certainty. In the experiment of hope in Jesus and his gospel they are open for the coming kingdom and experience its arrival already now in the acts of the Spirit. But the more sure they become through trust in the Father, the more they stand in solidarity with the groaning of the whole unredeemed world. In this hope, joy and agony are experienced simultaneously and in mutual intensity. Thus the experiment of hope leads them into temptation and to praying for deliverance from evil. Experiencing God and tempting God often exist side by side in the experiment of hope and are to be distinguished only in discipleship to Jesus and in remembrance of his passion. The experiment of hope is neither a certain nor an easy way, but it is the way of life in the midst of death. Not entering into it would mean not being ready to live at all in order to avoid the pain of disappointment as well as the happiness of love. Not entering into it would also be to act so as to avoid becoming guilty as well as being forgiven. Hope leads us into life, into the whole of life. It encourages faith so that it does not degenerate into faintheartedness. It strengthens love so that it does not remain enclosed within itself and with those who are like it. Thus Charles Péguy said:

> Hope leads everything.
> For faith only sees what *is*.
> But hope sees what *will be*.
> Charity only loves what *is*.
> But hope loves what will be—
> In time and for all eternity.[2]

The practical responsibility of Christian hope has not become easier in recent years. Of course the necessity of opening up new life and freedom for the hopeless, the hindered, the sick, the oppressed, and the guilty, is recognized everywhere. But the contradictions and adversaries are also growing apace. What we considered possible only a few years ago has been made impossible with violence. The practice of hope becames concretely stronger in suffering than in action and will have to be proved in resistance. The verse from the early poem of the unforgettable Ingeborg Bachmann is therefore more pertinent than ever:

> The uniform of the day is patience
> And its only decoration the pale star
> of hope over its heart. . . .
> It is awarded

for desertion,
for bravery in face of the friend,
for betraying all unworthy secrets
and the disregard of every command.

NOTES TO CHAPTER FOURTEEN

1. *The Star of Redemption, trans. William W. Hallo* (New York: Holt, Rinehart and Winston, 1971), p. 284.
2. *Mystère: Le Porche du Mystère de la Deuxième Vertu* (1911), in *Oeuvres Poétiques Complètes* (Paris: Editions Gallimard, 1957), pp. 539–540.